S.A.I.L.
Above
the Clouds

How to SIMPLIFY Your Life

A Sailor's lessons for uncovering inner strength, conquering chronic disease, and finding meaningful purpose.

First Edition

Book #1 of the S.A.I.L Series: Simplify, Align, Integrate, Let go

Carole Dion Fontaine

Inspired
CREATIONS
LLC

D0967538

ISBN 978-1-7361506-0-3 (Paperback Edition)
ISBN 978-1-7361506-1-0 (Ebook Edition)

Library of Congress Control Number: 2020922871

First Edition, 2020.

Editing: Sopurkha Kaur (Awareness Generation)

Cover and Book Design: Carole D. Fontaine

All Photographs © Carole D. Fontaine

Published by Inspired Creations, LLC
34 Memory Lane
Arundel, ME 04046

www.sailabovetheclouds.com

Printed in the United States of America.

*"May the winds of inspiration always keep
your sails and heart full!"*
—*Carole Fontaine*

Table of Contents

Acknowledgments

I want to thank many who have helped me bring this project to life, whether knowingly or by merely being a friend, mentor, or teacher.

First, I'd like to thank my loving husband, Eric, who's been so supportive of my quest for health, wellness, and spiritual journeying. Even though he does not always understand what I do, he has urged me to pursue what I love and seen firsthand how my life has transformed and how fulfilled this path has made me. Thank you for 30+ years of an unconventional life, adventures, personal growth challenges, and absolutely devoted love.

To my mom and dad, for being my constant cheering squad. Dad, your positivity through life's challenges has been the biggest lesson you have taught me. Mom, we are so alike and yet so different. My search for a better connection has been the source of so much growth and I could not have done this search without you. Thank you for being there for me, even when it felt challenging to understand me. I bless the day my soul chose both of you. Thanks for believing in me! I love you.

To Sat Sangat Kaur, my dear Belinda, who brought me to my first Kundalini Yoga Winter Solstice Celebration, I am so grateful! Thank you for being such a great friend and listener!

To Inder Kaur, for being a guide, teacher, and friend through a most painful period in my life. Thank you for giving me so much of your time, healing, and wisdom sharing—you've helped me understand myself, and the human condition. I cherish your gift of presence.

To Marianne, for helping me through one of the most painful experiences in my life and guiding me towards a clear and peaceful heart. Thank you for always having your "Carole radar" on. You are a gift to me. I love you.

To Neusa, for standing by me in the throes of transformation, seeing me through snot-nosed bawling sessions, thank you for your support and kind heart. I love you.

To Eve, for being an unofficial mentor to me, joined in our passions for sailing and healing, for your helpful sessions, meditations, and kind ear.

To Etta and Roz of the Brahma Kumaris of Hollywood, I am grateful for your impactful teachings and meditations. Your devotion sends waves of love throughout our community and me.

To Zayna, for booking my first Meditative Writing workshop at your studio, despite my insecurities. I'll always remember and appreciate the congratulatory note you sent to my husband which boosted how good I did. You rock. Je t'aime!

To SisterGoddessGoddess, for being an instigator, pot-stirrer, fence walker, limit pusher, and Goddess initiator, so much transformation has come from our journey together! Your eccentric, feminine, unique, playful, and sometimes messy way of unraveling us to re-emerge as the sister goddesses we are. What can I say but thank you, I love you.

To Jan, for your kind heart and supportive soul, thank you for your authenticity and for sharing my journey.

To my Sangat of Shakti sisters, soul sisters, Goddess sisters, who have grown, cried, loved, shared alongside, and continue to support me; your openness, vulnerability, and authenticity give me strength and inspiration.

To my Kundalini yoga spiritual community for being the one constant for unrivaled support, instant rejuvenation, actualization, unconditional love, and acceptance for who I am.

To my Gratitude Training family, for pushing me wayyyyyy beyond what I'd ever imagine possible, and for witnessing, and creating breakthroughs that helped me create my extraordinary life. I am because you are. 4 <3

To Aile Amana for sharing your Writing from the Heart™ practice with me years ago, which opened the door for me to develop my own practice.

To all my friends, teachers, and mentors who are too many to name but all have a special place in my heart, I dedicate this book to you.

To Guru Ram Das, you have my heart. Truth is my essence. Sat Nam!

Preface

It's been an eventful life so far, and I would not change a thing. From leaving our families and friends to move to another country, the financial stress and job insecurity, the car accidents, the years of sickness, painful surgeries, misdiagnosis and depressions (both mine and my husband's), the DUI, the bankruptcy of our sailing magazine—all the way to going back to a 9 to 5 job. As if all this weren't enough, we decided to add the daily challenges of two people (and a dog) living aboard a boat in tight quarters for 20 years.

As I breezed past my 50th birthday and reflected upon half of a century of life on the blue planet, I smiled at my unconventional life, adventures, and lessons learned. Just as the vessel I've lived on has been floating through life, I too have been bobbing away in my heart and mind, in a self-reflective state, grateful for the good and the bad to have brought such personal growth, shifts, and understanding.

Some say, "I would do it better," or, "If I had known, I would have never _____". But I only have gratefulness in my heart because every hard, challenging, and painful situation in my life brought me powerful lessons and made me uncover who I truly am and what I stand for.

What we do with the highs and lows in life defines who we are. How we adapt, grow and change to life's forever moving landscape is my definition of success, and I have probably had more opportunities to do so than if I wouldn't have jumped aboard a sailboat for a wild and wet 20-year ride.

The moment we stepped on board, two hippy bikers with very little money and barely any knowledge of sailing, set in motion the wheels of change in an exponential, torrential way.

I had to learn how to majorly downsize my life to fit in 41-foot of living space, and simplify all aspects of my life in order to make this a fun ride. (Both figuratively and literally!) I wet my guilds in this new floating lifestyle, and adapted everything in my day to day routine, figuring out how all the boat systems worked, and letting go of my attachment to material things, and the white picket fence "ideal" most of us grow up with. It wasn't always easy, especially living in tight quarters with someone who knows how to push your buttons! But the rewards of living life outside of the defined and expected far outweighed the limitations of space and growing pains.

I got to sail with pods of dolphins playing and jumping in our bow wake, explore deserted islands claiming it as our own, made friends with starfish and sea turtles, swam on remote beaches, and watched the moon rise miles away from land with only water and starry sky surrounding us from horizon to horizon, two souls and the Milky Way lighting our way. We bore witness to being ridiculously small, yet felt immensely connected to the Universe.

The uncomfortable became second nature and my ability to adapt to change grew. I watched my worries dissolve away in saltwater and immersed myself in the unknown. I found an inner strength I never knew existed. I listened to the ocean for her soothing sound and my heart expanded with the rewards of being fully engaged in captaining my own life.

Living 20 years on Windsong pushed me to grow beyond my imagination. The more immersed in nature I became, the more I journeyed into myself. It opened my heart to a spiritual world I had yet explored and propelled me into studying deep yogic philosophies, and healing modalities. Simplifying and stripping everything back to basic helped me develop and learn to trust my intuition, embrace all experiences as life lessons and gain tools to face immense personal challenges. All of which I used to surmount health crises, mental breakdowns, even survive our first hurricane.

There are so many meaningful events which had profound effects in my life and helped me get real, that I felt I needed to share these experiences in a book with the hope that it inspires you in some way to keep going, keep questioning, and growing—even when life gets hard. I hope this book helps you find what sets your soul on fire so you can gain the freedom to fully embrace yourself and express your gifts to the world. No matter how different you may feel you are, or no matter what sickness, dis-ease, or pain you may be experiencing, there is beauty in you and healing beyond where you may think your limitations exist.

If there is one thing that I found through sharing, it's that deep down, our hopes and fears are basically the same. Storytelling helps bridge the illusion that we are different and alone. When I connect and share an experience, I often see the light go off in someone's eyes—it's that moment when they realize we share the same pain. They know that if I can get through it, then they can get through it too. We can see and appreciate how our lives reflect and encourage each other to push on.

This book is meant to inspire you. You have full encouragement to laugh at my silliness, hold on through my adventures, celebrate my victories, and come out at the end with helpful tools, tips, and insights into a "salty" way of mindful living.

May you be brave, sail the unknown, and discover your path to Self-fulfillment.

Sat Nam, Namaste, Aho, Amen,
Happy sails,
Fair winds and following seas,

Carole Dion Fontaine
(Nam Karan Kaur)
S/v Windsong

How to get the most out of S.A.I.L. ABOVE THE CLOUDS

"If you want to sail above the clouds, you must first let go of the anchor that weighs you down." —Carole

S.A.I.L. Above the Clouds is a series of four books filled with stories and adventures from my 20 years of living on a sailboat with my husband. Each story illustrates a specific quest or lesson I learned on my path to healing my body from chronic disease, improving my relationship with myself and others, and finding the clarity I needed in my life to create inner peace and happiness. As we progress through the series, I dive deeper into emotional mastery and self-healing.

Each book represents an aspect and a letter in my S.A.I.L. program, designed to help you:

S = Simplify your life
A = Align your goals with purpose
I = Integrate tools for success
L = Let go of what doesn't serve you

…so you can create an extraordinary life.

Our inner landscape is a sea of hidden dreams, forgotten wishes, unconscious fears, deeply ingrained habits, and mind-boggling blockages. Amid all the dramas in our lives, each one of us carries the answers to all our challenges inside of us. Like a treasure chest buried deep at the bottom of the sea, we hold the key to infinite possibilities of health, success, and abundance.

But to get to the treasure, we must set sail on a journey that will bring us to a new landscape—an inner landscape. Nothing of value was ever found without a bit of courage and bravery. Just as I have sailed towards and through the unknown, the sharing of my humor-filled and deeply healing adventures is intended to help you sail on an inner journey to:

- clear out rubbish that's blocking your way,
- establish goals you mean to attain,
- discover tools you can use to reach those goals and
- let go of the fears that's clouding your freedom to step into your greatness and beyond.

You see, when we SIMPLIFY our lives, pathways and solutions become clear. We can then ALIGN ourselves with our highest goals, INTEGRATING tools which support healing and success so that we can LET GO of fears and blockages, and be free to embody our dreams.

The goal is to get people unstuck, inspired, energized, connected with their bodies, pro-active towards healing their bodies, engaged in elevating their lives, and realizing that they always have a choice.

Following each chapter, you will find exercises to help you observe, question, reflect, and grow. It is designed to help you gain insights into your life like clues on a treasure map.

My ultimate goal is to show you a path where you can SAIL ABOVE THE CLOUDS, no matter what ails you, or what situation you face, you can move past these obstacles and meet them with a clear, sharp mind and a peaceful heart. Imagine living life where you feel able to speak your truth in flourishing relationships, pursue your dreams with passion, and embody health and success no matter what life throws at you. Give yourself permission to go on this treasure hunt. Rally the curious child within, and put on your explorer's hat. This may be the greatest adventure you'll ever take!

Each chapter contains:

ADVENTURE: My stories progress through time, but do not necessarily follow one another.

 LESSON: The lesson I learned.

QUESTION: A Meditative Writing question.

If you want to get the most out of my books, be ready with a pen and paper to answer the writing prompts after each chapter. *(A journaling section has been provided for you at the end of the book.)* Journaling will give you the greatest insights into how to bring your life to the next level. You have deep wisdom inside of you that is untapped or blocked behind unconscious limiting beliefs. Answer the writing prompts as honestly as you can, with the first thought that comes to mind. It is imperative that you do not edit and use only these first thoughts, no matter how embarrassing, rude, or shocking they may be.

First thoughts have tremendous power and come directly from an unedited source, before our mind restricts, confine, judge, or polish them. It is essential to air out these thoughts to:

1) Clear out your mind,
2) Take away the power these thoughts may have on you,
3) Discover what truly is at the source of your blockages,
4) Tap into your inner wisdom to improve your life,
5) Formulate a plan to reach your goals.

This practice will help you notice, understand, and change detrimental behaviors, habits, or negative self-talk. It can be exceptionally healing and life-changing if you allow it. Trust in the process. Permit yourself to let anything come up without judgment, and be compassionate towards yourself.

Take it one step further by setting up a timer on 5 minutes and write continuously until the bell rings. Do not stop, or allow yourself time to think about your answer, and surprise yourself with the words that will pour out of you. Do not reread, cross out, or bother with grammar, just write uninterrupted for 5 minutes (or more). If you do not know what to write, simply write, "I don't know what to write" until something comes to mind, or the time is up. It is part of the process to work on the resistance you may feel on certain subjects.

 ACTION: A simple exercise to bring awareness, mindfulness, and success into your day to day life.

MEDITATION DOWNLOAD: Each of the four books includes one free meditation you can download and practice whenever you feel moved to do so. Visit www.SailAboveTheClouds.com to download.

I cannot praise the benefits of meditation enough. If you are a beginner, think about it as a daily time investment that will help you realize your goals and dreams. To have a healthy body you need to exercise everyday. Think of meditation as exercising your brain muscles. It works. Science now agrees that having a mindfulness practice will not only raise your quality of life but can also extend it. People who meditate see their creativity improve, feel more relaxed and reduce symptoms of stress, anxiety and depression.

A John Hopkins study proved that meditation rivaled the effects of anti-depressants [1], while UCLA showed evidence that long-term meditators have better-preserved brains as they aged. [2] A study at Yale University proved that meditation does in fact allow individuals to be more present and aware, so they have better focus and a clearer, calmer mind [3].

Who doesn't want to live a healthier, happier, longer life?
Sail on sailor!

Disclaimer

Carole Fontaine is a certified Life Coach. Tips and techniques in this book are offered as tools for a healthier and happier lifestyle. Please refer to a therapist or health care specialist for personal or medical challenges you may be experiencing.

S = SIMPLIFY YOUR LIFE

---

sim·pli·fy: make (something) simpler or easier to do or understand.

My first step to help you
S.A.I.L. Above the Clouds
is SIMPLIFY.

We cannot rise above life's cloudy moments if we carry unnecessary burdens on our back. This may appear in our life as clutter, habits, unconscious behaviors, or superficial stuff that is eating up space in our mind, home, heart, and career. Even if we don't see it or know about it, these things can swallow our precious energy which is better spent healing ourselves, navigating life's daily challenges, and creating our extraordinary life.

When I moved aboard Windsong, I had no choice but to declutter my life in order to squeeze all that I had into a small living space. The declutter process caused such a drastic shift in my perception of life. I realized the clutter was acting as a blindfold that hid me from my own internal spaces. This inspired me to look at how to get rid of my emotional clutter too. Life was complicated enough without adding more drama to it from being caught up in my own stories, ego-mind, and fears. So, my first quest was to simplify my life and get back to basics.

Learning to remove my blindfolds helped me see through the clouds of resistance I had been nurturing, so that I could realign my unfocused energy. Simplifying meant removing needless suffering and gaining a newfound clarity. Since distractions and obstacles were being removed or simplified, it helped me problem solve and resolve. Furthermore, it helped me connect with my inner essence and get clear on my heart's purpose and what I needed to do to heal and find joy.

So let's dive into Simplify, and learn how living simply can teach us to simply live.

Introduction

They say the best days in a boater's life are the day they buy their boat and the day they sell it. I can vouch for the first, but we haven't sold Windsong yet, although it's on the horizon after 22 years.

All those many days in between represent knotted lines, scrapped shallow bottoms, unexpected adventures, and encountered storms. Through it all, both my husband Eric and I have grown, learned, and become highly attuned individuals in the ways of life, relationships, and sailing.

I hope this inspires you to take the helm of your own life and steer towards peaceful seas. May you find the courage to ride out your storm until the sun comes out again. For it always does.

1. Triggers—and Naked Strangers

Simplify your Questions

"If you never dive in, you'll never discover the sea of possibilities." —Carole

It was spring 1997, and we were witnessing the sun slowly setting down on Dania Beach. We were badly hungover and disheveled from the night before, our motorcycles parked just a few feet away. Still a bit dazed from a particularly badass party at our house where the music ran all night till dawn, I remember thinking to myself, "I can't do this anymore." We'd been living life on the edge: partying hard, drinking until the wee hours of the morning, smoking, taking recreational drugs, and hammering a crazy lifestyle for longer than I could remember. I was still pissed off at the half-naked girl I met at 3 am who was swimming in my pool. Very drunk, she'd look up and say, "Who are you?" in a belligerent kind of way. We had an entourage of good friends, but also some stragglers and profiteers who often crashed our popular after-hour parties. Unbeknownst to her–she'd just smacked my world upside down with this one simple question.

Who was I? What had I become? What was I doing? Is this who I wanted to be? Is this what I wanted to do with my life?

We'd been acting like rockstars, burning the candle at both ends— and my light was burning out. My life revolved around the next party, the next drink, the next joint, and I was losing my husband to a bottle of Jack Daniels whiskey. I was 27. We'd immigrated to the U.S. from

Canada just three years earlier, and I hadn't been doing anything with my life except hanging out poolside with my girlfriends and sipping margaritas. The party crasher's innocent question was a trigger that hit a raw nerve and sent sparks down my soul.

So it was. My husband and I found ourselves sitting at the beach in the sand, staring at the boats sailing in and out of Port Everglades. The Florida dream we'd worked so hard to achieve didn't feel good anymore. Our hearts heavy with day-after regrets of things done, and words said.

We turned our gaze to the water to find peace.

Here, we could relax and talk openly. I shared that I couldn't live like this anymore, I was suffocating, and everything felt out of control. Eric had recently gotten a DUI and spent the night in jail, which had scared the heck out of us, and opened our eyes to our reckless ways. We had been acting like careless jaded kids. And what do kids do when they're bored? They do stupid things.

We sat and talked.

Florida, we had found, was too hot to ride our motorcycles. We had moved here for the year-round riding weather, but the scenery we were used to in Canada, like long winding roads, with hills and countryside were non-existent, and our thick Canadian blood couldn't handle a hot motor melting us in the 95-degree weather. So we spent our time by the enormous pool in our backyard, cooling our brains, and jumping into the deep end. The water was amazing and a necessity for new overheated Floridians, but the real attraction was the ocean. We'd never lived close to her, and she was captivating. Even in our party days, she called on us like a distant echo, repeating her longing message of a soothing return to nature. But I had long ago tuned out any inner voice that sent even a glimpse of discontent in my mind.

We were so used to avoidance and numbing out, that our reality had become a grand illusion. On the outside, we were the happiest couple with the biggest house, best parties, and successful life, but on the inside, we were disconnected, lost, and longing for something meaningful.

I remember being very nervous about telling my husband how I felt, scared that my feelings would not be reciprocated, scared that by sharing how I truly felt behind our facade, I would cause an even greater rift between us. But I was waking up to my very unhappy self, and now that I was listening, I could not stop hearing the screams inside my head.

It felt good to confide in him, and I realized that we both felt like there must be something else to life than this. By opening up to Eric, he then felt comfortable opening up to me! Come to find out, he was tired and bored with the routine and felt stuck. The constant parties were his way of numbing out the pressure he'd been under to sustain our lifestyle. We rarely paused and asked ourselves how we were feeling. I think this may have been the first time that we ever sat and talked about deep feelings, and made a conscious decision together to change our lives.

Our move from Canada to the US had been a total impulse— unplanned and surrounded by crazy mayhem from two careless young adults. We broke a 2-year lease we had just signed on a house and Eric ran off to find a job in Florida, driving away with a packed army bag tied to the back of his motorcycle three days before the first snowstorm arrived. I stayed behind to sell off, give away, and pack our belongings before joining him. The first five years we had been together was basically one never-ending party, sometimes paused by the little things in life, you know, like immigrating, finding a job, resettling, getting married, starting a new life in a new country, etc., and it seemed life was catching up to us.

Now that we had gotten our feelings out in the open, the tension eased. The sound of the waves caressing the shore was comforting. We felt connected again. There is something magical and healing about the ocean. We just sat there taking it all in, the blue sky, the salty air, the sound of the seagulls, the fishing pier in the distance. We had kicked off our riding boots and dug our feet in the sand, the warmth of it running through our toes was heartwarming. The everlasting waves of Mother Ocean moved in and out every minute, every hour, every day, always caressing our shores just a footstep away, calling us and reminding us to never stop moving forward, no matter what. Somehow those waves encouraged us with the notion that there are shores yet unseen, depths unexplored, opportunities undiscovered, and that if we looked deeper, we would see that Mother Ocean carried an unlimited potential for life inside of her. Then it hit me. So—did—we! I felt uplifted and excited for the first time in a long time.

It's like we had hit the pause button on our crazy life and were briefly suspended in a moment of clarity. We loved each other, we didn't like what we were becoming, and we needed change. The rhythm of the waves soothed us. Between pauses of silence, we talked about our future.

That's when Eric spotted a small boat, barely larger than a canoe, dancing around the waves outside the inlet. "We could get a boat!" he offered.

"Hmmm…" I replied, "What kind of boat?"

"Something small that we could go take rides in and would be easy to trailer, but big enough that we could go out there like this boat, on the ocean!" He said, smiling.

"Sure, why not?" I replied. I'd never been on the ocean, but I was willing to try anything to change this uneasy feeling and clear out the brain fog.

"Did you ever sail a boat?" I asked.

"When I was a kid, I had a canoe on the lake, and my grandma let me drive her pontoon when we went fishing." Eric recalled.

That was good enough for me. After all, I had moved 1,600 miles to a different country to continue life with this crazy, adorable man, so getting a boat would be just another small step on our adventure, right?

Right then and there, in the steamy sand of Dania Beach, a dream took shape, and we first glanced at our new beginning.

 LESSON: Simplify your questions. When the short and direct question, "Who are you?" shifted my whole perspective and sent me on a new lifelong path of searching for answers, it also made me appreciate the power of conversation and asking the right questions.

I was so busy living my life "out there" that I had forgotten to look within and ask myself how I was feeling. In those days, my conversations with self and others were mostly superficial and avoided any and all subjects that might raise questions, or, 'rock the boat.' I ignored painful conversations until I was at the breaking point, choosing to bury myself with the busyness of life.

You cannot be clear in your conversation with others if your mind is unclear on what you want and what you stand for. Remedy that by having a continuous dialogue with your inner self, asking the hard questions, and knowing yourself—before a half-naked stranger stumps you in your pool!

Humans aren't mind readers, and communication is key to having healthy relationships. Forego meaningless conversations and make your questions count. Your next conversation could potentially be a catalyst for someone else. Learn to express yourself clearly and directly with the world outside, and be straight and precise in expressing your needs. It's a practice worth incorporating; you can take my word!

QUESTION: Some of the qualities and talents I possess are (write down at least 10)...

Then answer the following by writing for 5 minutes each time you answer the question. Allow whatever comes up to be expressed:
1. Who am I?
2. Who am I?
3. Who am I?

 ACTION: Change your elevator speech

The next time someone asks you, "Who are you? Or, "What do you do?" Answer using the qualities and talents you just wrote down and observe how wonderfully the tone of the conversation changes.

In your conversations, instead of asking people what work they do, ask what their gifts and talents are and watch their eyes light up as they share qualities. If someone does not know how to answer, you then become an ambassador to help this person discover their gifts. This is a useful and powerful way to start new friendships!

2. Ahoy Mate—
I "wannabe" a sailor

Simplify your Search

"Master your own ship, and let go of the fleet." —Carole

"Wannabe" was the name of our first sailboat. We traded our helmets, leathers, and riding boots; for straw hats, swimsuits and flip-flops. We decided to call it "Wannabe" because we wanted-to-be sailors! We invited some of our friends to witness our "boat renaming" ceremony, with the obligatory breaking of a champagne bottle on the bow (the front tip of the boat). It was all done in great fun, but we'd been warned about the myth around renaming vessels; should you leave any item on the ship with the old name written on it, or forget to stamp out or erase mention of the old name anywhere, you would suffer the great wrath of the angered Sea Gods and be forever cursed with infinite bad luck. We took it seriously and weren't about to risk it, so we blacked out, tore up, and removed any mention of its past identity.

It took a couple of tries to baptize Wannabe. Surprisingly, it's tough to break a champagne bottle on the bow of a boat! But we finally did it, ruining the champagne with broken glass in it, but the deed was done. We raised our glasses filled with rum to celebrate its rebirth and a birthing of our new hobby.

While Eric had some boating experience from living by a lake as a kid, I was a greenhorn. I may have been in a canoe at summer camp, and taken a boat ride once on a family vacation. I didn't even know if I would get seasick, but I had an adventurous spirit.

It only took us six weeks to take the plunge. Eric convinced me that a small sailboat, which had an enclosed cabin, and a head (nautical term for toilet), was a much better buy for a few hundred dollars more than an open boat. I sold my beloved Harley Davidson with a mix of sadness and excitement and paid for the day sailor.

We were the proud owners of a used 25 foot MacGregor, with pop up top and swing keel—complete with trailer. It was such an exciting day! I remember feeling such elation at owning a boat. Not having a damn clue as to how we were supposed to sail it, but loving the romantic lines of it, the feel of the tiller, playing with the strange hardware, seeing the miniature kitchen and cabin we would stay in, even smelling the moldy boat scent made me giddy! Adventures were on the horizon.

It was a bit run down and needed some repairs, so Eric spent all the free time he had for the next six weeks, sanding, waxing, rewiring, and making the boat seaworthy again. He poured so much love, sweat, and even some blood into Wannabe for good measure. It wasn't much, but it was ours, and we intended to sail the heck out of it.

If life, as we know it until now, didn't make us happy, then we would do anything in our power to find out what would. And this was our first attempt at answering that question: Who do you want to be?

 LESSON: Simplify your search. What do you do when you're lost? You ask for guidance. What do you do when you feel stuck, and don't know what to do? You pause and look for answers. If you don't like who or where you are in life, get out of your way, go in and find out what you want. Your search for solutions to challenges or for what makes you happy starts by asking yourself basic questions. You don't need to sign up for 50 different courses, buy all the self-help books (including mine!), and ask all your peers for their opinions. All you need is to get to know yourself.

What you like or dislike may not be the same things as last year or even a few months ago. Get to know the real you. Ask yourself simple and direct questions, and listen deeply for an honest, soulful reply. Make sure you check in with yourself regularly and search for what keeps you in a state of joy.

Awareness and self-inquiry will unearth the answers you seek and create clarity in your life. You won't get answers if you don't ask, and you must pause long enough to hear the answers.

The most straightforward questions are sometimes the hardest to answer, but the insights you'll get from these answers will benefit you and point your compass the right way. Put the timer on for at least five minutes per question and write non-stop, answering these simple questions:

QUESTION: Who do I want to be? What do I want?

What do I like? What do I not like?

 ACTION: Get a journal
If that wasn't clear enough, get a journal and unleash the sails of your heart!

3. Storming, Dragging, and Fireworks—So it Begins

Simplify your Skills

"No storm, no rainbow." —Carole

Wannabe was a sporty little trailerable boat, so we took it everywhere. That summer was a funfest. We traveled up and down the Florida coast, leaving early in the morning, looking for boat ramps to dip Wannabe in and go play. It was equipped with the basics so that we could spend the night and sail back the next day. It had a tiny cabin: on one side, there were two seats and a small table, on the other, it had the cutest tiny sink and small countertop which acted as the kitchen. The top popped up a few feet to give your head room to walk around when you were at anchor. If you ventured farther into the haul, to the right, you found an enclosed head, with a pump marine toilet, and in the bow, or tip of the boat, you had the v-berth, with a bed shaped like the V of the front of the boat. It had hammocks on the side to hold our stuff, and tiny portholes to look outside.

It was a great boat to learn how to sail. Small and light, when we ran aground, Eric called everybody off the boat, and as soon as we'd jump in the water, the little boat would float up, Eric would lift up the centerboard*, and we'd push it off the sandbar. It handled like a toy and was very forgiving.

*(A centerboard is a long narrow board (keel) used to prevent drifting. It projects downward to provide lateral resistance and help steady the boat. Ours was retractable and you could pivot it in and out of a slot at the bottom of the boat (hull) with a small mechanical device (winch) giving the boat more "grip" in the water.)

Every week we'd get more confident. We had to step up the mast (raise and secure the tall upright post that carries the sails) at the boat ramp, and tie it up before going in the water, and then lower it when we came back, securing it before hitting the road.

My job was to handle the sails, while Eric was captain and navigator. I learned everything about it and loved to put on my gloves and haul that sail up. The sound of it climbing up the sail track, the sail lightly flopping in the wind waiting for the wind to fully engulf and run its sheet, the excitement building in my gut, and joy at being out on the water. Once the sail was all the way up, I would give the captain the signal to ease the boat into the wind. (You always raise and lower the sails when the boat points into the wind, it is the neutral position, so that your sails are empty and can be maneuvered up and down more easily, without causing stress or damage.)

Eric would ease that baby into the wind, and we'd slowly take off. When we heeled to the wind and shut the little motor down, it was like we entered a new world, away from the hustle and bustle, and suspended in silence. We had never experienced anything like this before and were instantly hooked.

We practiced in bays and shallow waters for a while, familiarizing ourselves with the sport of sailing.

The first day we decided to sail out of Biscayne Bay to try our hands at coastal ocean sailing was June 22, 1997. Mother Ocean sent us home dripping wet, with our tails between our legs (literally for our very unhappy wet dog). The thing with small boats is that they're very light and easily drift, so waves can send them flying every which way. Although you may think boats are fast, they're not fast enough to outrun a tropical downpour—contrary to what my husband believed at the time.

Biscayne Bay is a lagoon that is about 35 miles long and 8 miles wide, located directly South of Miami Beach. It is enclosed oceanside by miles of shallow sandy flats, and a range of islands called Keys or Cays, which together separates the bay from the ocean waters. This creates a protective barrier against rough seas and larger waves and is the perfect place to learn how to sail. It's like a large lake for adults with big toys.

It's also a designated aquatic preserve, and every time I've sailed Biscayne Bay, I've always been blessed to see bottlenose dolphins, often riding our bow wake.

For newbies like us, 428 square miles of approximately 15 feet water, was an impressive playground, especially considering it was the first time in our lives that we were going to be sleeping and floating on a boat. We loved the feeling of security provided by the closeness of the beach and city, and at the same time, we were completely removed from the craziness of Miami life. We felt like invisible spectators free to roam behind the scenes and observe without being seen.

Sunday, June 22, 1997

It was a typical hot Florida summer day, one where you can only be outdoors if in a bikini by the pool or at the beach—this was a beautiful day in paradise; brilliant sun and perfect blue sky. We'd chosen this weekend to be our first official overnight stay on Wannabe. Our friend Wizard, who had some sailing experience, joined us for the inauguration. He was a small catamaran sailor and sailed his Sunseeker regularly on Biscayne Bay.

We launched Wannabe at Crandon Park's boat ramp. Dingo, our dog at the time, was on board but very suspicious of mom and dad's new hobby. Cooler, towels, sunscreen and drinks were thrown in the small vessel, and we waved goodbye to shore, raising the sail, with stories of pirates and great explorers fresh in our minds and the strong unfamiliar salty air filling our lungs.

We thought we were the bomb and the cat's meow sliding into the water, sails flying high, moving towards the great unknown with impeccable flair. After a few hours of tacking away in the bay, (maneuvering our boat in zig zags so that the sails are always filled and propelling us onward despite having the wind in our face), our confidence purred up, and we decided to aim for the great big blue beyond the reef, where the ocean awaited. "Why not?" We asked ourselves. We had everything under control and felt very confident. Of course, we thought we were ready, "There's nothing to this, we've got this!"

At the speed our small sailboat was going, it took more than an hour to get around the peninsula and reach the start of the deeper water. The moment we patted ourselves on the back for thinking we were "real sailors," we turned around and saw dark, ominous clouds forming on the horizon.

The guys weren't too worried about it and were caught up in the fun of their new toy, pushing on, tweaking the sail, gaining speed, so we stayed on course for a while.

As soon as we made it out to sea, the sun disappeared. The clouds rallied up at incredible speed, and a rumble was heard in the distance. A tropical downpour was on the way.

As inexperienced sailors, one thing we didn't know yet, is that storms on the water can turn nasty very quickly. An experienced sailor is one who has learned to read the movement of the wind and clouds, and knows to make preparations, or take cover the moment the wind shifts direction and the temperature drops.

Within minutes of guessing that it would veer the other way, clouds covered the sun and it got dark, cold, and windy. A violent wind rolled in from the opposite direction, circled our little boat, and sent us flying. We were thrown sideways by the force of it. Before I could rescue

Dingo, who had fallen below, a downpour fell on us. Our little Wannabe daysailer was captured by turbulent winds, and thrown around like a toy. The waves started to build up. Mayhem reigned on board, while I rushed to secure the dog, and the guys tried to get the boat under control. They started the little motor. Wizard held the tiller all the way to starboard (that's to the right, in nautical terms) to turn us around. Eric ran up front to grab the sails and pull them down before they ripped. It took all of his strength and balance to hold on, and not get thrown off the little boat while the lines slapped at him in a fury as he tried to grasp the flapping sail.

Wizard's efforts on the tiller did not affect the boat's direction whatsoever; he tried port side (left), he tried starboard side, but the small MacGregor completely lacked enough weight to provide stability to our little boat and give the oncoming winds a match worth fighting for. We were like a spinning toy in the hands of Neptune. It was too far to swim to the coast if we sank, and we remained at the mercy of a weather system, still confused and surprised at the quickness of its unraveling.

At that moment, Eric thought to himself, "If I get out of this, and make it home, I'M SELLING THIS DAMN BOAT."

It took what seemed like hours for the guys to get the boat under control and aim it back towards the bay. But we know it was only minutes. The storm didn't do any damage except to our inflated egos. We crawled back at turtle speed to the safety of Biscayne Bay, drenched like our dog.

By four o'clock, we were finally anchored in front of Hobie Beach. We cracked open a cold one and got over our emotions. We laughed at having survived our first water encounter with Florida's daily afternoon thunderstorm.

The postcard view of the Miami skyline blending with the shore, palm trees, and beach, was one of the most beautiful things I had ever seen. We pivoted our focus to our inaugural and well-earned dinner, featuring the biggest steaks we could find at the store (that was when I still ate beef). The captain-turned-chef grilled them on our miniature BBQ which he tied to the boat's railing. We all joked about whether he made sure the screws were on tight so that it wouldn't fall in the water with our dinner. We almost lost a steak, but Eric once again came through on his duty!

Despite the afternoon emotions, one could not help but feel very blessed to be here. Not a lot of people get to enjoy this magical side of Miami. We watched the sunset behind the glamorous city, and felt lucky to be alive, to witness such beauty, and felt enamored with life.

As the night turned dark, and the city lights blinked on, fireworks suddenly blasted the sky. Tons of them, of all colors, high and low, loud ones and fizzle ones. Wow. It was the perfect bang after our explosive day. We were blissed out and absolutely thrilled with our day. What a difference today had been compared to just a few months ago when we were at the end of our rope, sitting on the beach hungover, and trying to figure our lives. Oh, how we loved our new toy! Eric decided then and there that he wouldn't sell the boat after all, he'd give Wannabe another chance. It was only years later that he told me how he'd felt in the middle of the storm. He confessed that there was a moment when he realized that he had no clue what to do and was truly unprepared to face the elements. With a sinking feeling at the bottom of his stomach, he felt he was going to die and take his wife and dog along with him. He swore that he would never put his family in this dangerous kind of situation and that if we'd make it back to shore that he was going to sell the damn boat.

I'm glad he didn't follow through and that our bad day ended on a high note. We'd just had a tiny taste of the adventures that awaited us and discovered newfound respect for Mother Nature.

We stayed up watching the stars overhead and relaxed into the darkness of the bay. The sound from the city was dulled out and we could admire its beauty like a silent witness, spying in the night. We hadn't been this close to nature in a very long time, and it was inebriating—in the best sense, not the Jack Daniels kind this time.

When we got ready for bed, we accidentally dropped the cabin door in the water. We weren't used to being on a boat yet. Things would easily find themselves overboard in those early years! It was too dark to fetch it, so we decided to dive for it in the morning. We fell into luxurious sleep in the only room below tucked in the pointy tip of the boat (bow), and Wizard upstairs, sleeping under the stars. It was strange to sleep aboard a floating boat. Everything moved, and the sound through the hull was very echoey. But somehow, the motion felt very soothing.

We woke up at dawn to find that we had traveled about three football fields to the west. We were now anchored farther from the beach, and close to the busy channel. You're not supposed to travel when you're sleeping at anchor! It could have been disastrous. Lucky for us, we were surrounded by miles of bay, a sandy beach, and a guardian angel had been watching over us.

We learned the importance of setting a good anchor before retiring for the night and making sure we were well-grounded before leaving watch. And since we had moved so far from our original spot, it took us a while, but after a few dives, we finally found the lost door!

 LESSON: Simplify your skills. If you want to realize a dream, you will most likely need to gain some knowledge and skills to get there. Start at the bottom and educate yourself as to everything you need to know and acquire to reach your goal. Learn to master each step before moving on to the next phase. Building a strong foundation will assure safety in the most dire situation and help you withstand storms in unpredictable weather. Following that weekend, we signed up for the Coast Guard Auxiliary courses and learned basic boat safety and advanced navigation. We spent the next few years mastering the art of sailing.

One of the most important things we learned on the bay that day (besides respecting the weather and the sea) was learning to anchor ourselves so we would not drift at the first sign of waves rocking our boat. When you are not adequately grounded or anchored in life, you find yourself drifting at the first sign of pressure, often without realizing it before it's too late. It is a potentially dangerous situation that can leave you lost and shipwrecked. Grounding yourself in life, as well as at sea, will save you much stress. You can achieve this by identifying the basic tools and knowledge that you need to help you be your best.

QUESTION: What makes me feel out of control?
What makes me feel secure?

ACTION: Earthing

If you feel disconnected, insecure, depressed, unclear, out of control, or if you suffer from insomnia, chronic pain, or any kind of inflammatory disease—try walking barefoot on the grass for 10 minutes. This will connect you directly to the earth. Without shoes, you'll be able to ground yourself and receive free electrons that will be transferred throughout your body. It's called *Earthing* and it has an array of health benefits, and it's free!

In biology 101, most of us learned how free radicals damage healthy cells in the body and that taking antioxidants will help neutralize these negative effects. The antioxidant actually donates electrons to the free radical, quenching its thirst for the missing electron. Once grounded, the free radical no longer contributes to inflammation in the body.

The same happens when you walk barefoot and connect to the surface of the earth which is made up of negative electrons. They have the ability to move freely and when in contact with human tissue, can equalize and reduce the positive charge—aka free radicals. Just another free gift from Mother Earth.

Bonus points if you can recall the feeling you got from running barefoot outside when you were a kid!

4. Buying Windsong—Yes, We're Doing This!

Simplify your Attitude

"I'll risk it all for sailing a rainbow." —Carole

I remember the day clearly. It was months later when Eric walked into the house with a sheepish look on his face…you know, the sugary eyes a boy gives you when he's not quite sure if he's in trouble, but wants to sweeten you up before he tells you his story just in case? I knew we were about to have a big conversation. The last time I'd seen that look, we had moved from one country to another.

"I want to buy a large sailboat and live on it," he said. Wow, like I hadn't seen this one coming (I'm being sarcastic here)? We had just spent the most exciting summer, bumming around South Florida and the Florida Keys on Wannabe. Our first ever sailing vacation had sealed the deal—we were in love with boating!

Everything about boating was fun for us. It was so easy to trailer this small boat that we'd search boat ramps and launch it on every ramp south of Fort Lauderdale. We discovered bays, lakes, lagoons, hidden anchorages, stunning views, deserted islands, party isles, and were fast becoming nature addicts. Wannabe was not the best toy to sail the deeper ocean waters, but on a good day, this boat was a hoot! We'd been exploring the shallower more protected waters up and down the coast.

We spent two weeks sailing the Florida Keys (a chain of islands at the south west tip of Florida extending approx. 120 miles), exploring the Florida Bay into the Gulf of Mexico, and sailing down to Key West. The trip was outstanding. It was just the two of us and Dingo the dog. On both weekends, friends joined us for an overnighter, we played and sailed all day, grilled fantastic meals on our tiny BBQ, and they slept outside under the stars because the little boat was too small to hold everyone in the cabin. To this day, we all remember those days with a warm fuzzy feeling in our hearts. It was the first time we saw wild dolphins up close, or anchored and walked on deserted islands surrounded by beaches rarely a soul had walked. We realized that life was much grander than we had thought; our small world was expanding.

We made a few overnight stays in marinas mostly to recharge our battery, fill our water tank, and refuel our little motor we used to get in and out of anchorages. The first time we came out with our orange home extension cord to plug the boat and charge our batteries, Eric realized that it did not fit in the marina outlet. He searched, and all the docking stations had the same connection. Curious onlooking neighbors explained that boats did not have the same power extension outlet connector, we needed an adapter. One neighbor said he had one to loan us, and another other jumped off his boat and helped us connect it. This was the first time we met 'liveaboard' boaters. We had rarely met such a friendly, welcoming bunch so eager to help. They duct taped our extension to the dock so no one would trip over it, and invited us aboard for cocktails. They told us that when they'd seen us pull in sunburned, chapped lips, and with huge grins on our faces, they'd predicted we would soon move onto a larger boat.

Unbeknownst to them, they foretold our future. Fast forward six months later, and here was Eric in front of me, pleading his case.

We had been together seven years at the time, and I knew Eric pretty well and figured that this was where we were headed. We were young, new to this country, Eric had his work permit and worked for Harley Davidson of Miami, but I was still not allowed to work until we got our green cards. We had only been in the US for a short time, so we were not tied down too much, and after making that risky move, I was game to trying new things.

But we had no credit history in the US and nothing of value in our name. It was a big dream to jump in, and the financial responsibility would fall entirely on him until I was allowed to work.

He promised to make every payment, even if it meant that he would eat peanut butter for a month (or did he say Cheez Whiz?). He always had a flair for drama! It was a huge commitment and investment for us. Since we were not American citizens yet, the only bank loan we could get was at 10.75% financing because we were considered a flight risk. For such a big-ticket item, that's a shitload of money just going toward interest.

Our wildest friends were super excited for us, but I think most of our family had doubts about our decisions and life choices at the time. Some showed good faith, shrugged their shoulders and thought, "Here they go again."

So, I said, "YES." It was a risk I was willing to take. If something happened and we couldn't afford the payments, then the bank would take it back. This was a gamble we were ready to make.

In the last three years since our move to Florida we made a very comfortable home out of almost nothing, and established a short yet decent credit history. This provided me with security, however misplaced, and had been a comforting feeling after the fears and gripping doubts I'd experienced when I drove down to Florida alone with just the stuff that could fit in a van to meet up with Eric. I hadn't expected to start over again so soon and be asked to leave the familiar for the unknown—AGAIN—and risk losing what little we had, but I felt that it was a worthy adventure even with the nervous butterflies in my stomach.

Besides, I was still in my audacious twenties; no risk, no victory! It felt so right and true; there was no way we weren't going to go for it.

Surprisingly, from the moment we decided to jump, all obstacles fell away. Because of our immigration status, no banks would loan us for a boat. A friend of Eric's boss was in finance, and after he made Eric promise he would make good on the loan, he approved us for a high-interest boat loan. We only shopped for a few weeks and only visited three other sailboats when the magic happened.

At the time, the only thing we owned was our 25-foot Wannabe sailboat, it's trailer, and a stunning custom-painted van with murals of pirates and engraved windows to tow it. Eric still had his Harley, which he'd put up for sale to get the cash down payment. He'd been eagerly scanning the Boat Trader every week. In the third week, a new ad appeared: "1981, 41 Morgan OutIslander sailboat, looking to trade down to a smaller sailboat with trailer and van..." I kid you not. Sight unseen, this was our boat, we just knew it.

We called Captain Don that day and agreed to drive up to Lake Okeechobee the following Saturday to visit. We hit it off right away. He was a jolly good fellow who had been sailing Windsong on the freshwater lake for over ten years. He was aging and wanted something easier to maneuver. We fell in love with Windsong's lines as soon as we set foot on the dock. It was a beauty with its coral blue canvas and white hull.

We were such newbies, but our hearts told us that we belonged together and that Windsong would take us on a lot of adventures. I'm sure glad those crazy young kids went for it. On December 4, 1997, we became the proud owners of a 41-foot Morgan OutIslander 416 Ketch.

La chanson du vent…the song of the wind. The name was perfect. We felt an irresistible calling coming from the depth of our souls. A soulful wind that would sweep across our lives and propel us toward an incredible journey. We would keep this name and honor it thoroughly.

LESSON: Simplify your attitude. One of the things I love the most about my husband is that he is not afraid of taking risks. If I hadn't been with him, I swear I'd still be in Canada, never having done half the things we did, especially buy a boat and live on it for 20+ years! He has the attitude of a go-getter.

Me, I'm a homebody by nature, and a bit more fearful and careful, but I chose to have a positive attitude and always look for the brighter side of things. If I tap into my feelings, I can get mixed signals that can be confusing, frustrating and even scary. Uncomfortableness can be both exciting and scary at the same time. Does it mean that it's bad? No!

I simplify it by asking myself, "Do these feelings come from love or fear?" It's that simple!

For example, how does 'moving to Florida' feel in my body? Overwhelming but also exciting, I choose exciting!

'Let's buy an expensive boat and live on it!' How does that feel in my body? Scary but the underlying feeling of adventure thrills me. I choose adventure!

I do have fears, but I keep them in check and expect good things to happen. I've always looked at the silver lining. Maybe I inherited it from my positively cheerful dad. It's a practice that has helped me through a lot. I can do anything I want to do, with the right attitude. I can choose to grow, change, move, and learn new things every single day. I don't ignore negative emotions but I do disregard the unsubstantiated fears that may keep me stuck. Yes, some days I fall into a negative attitude, but with a strong personal practice, I can stay centered and get back to my constructive approach to life.

I know a lot of people didn't believe in us in the beginning, and that's ok. I chose not to let everybody's concerns or bad mojo change my attitude of, "Let's do it!" I'm not a risk-taker by nature, but I teach myself every day to sail outside my comfort zone, and guess what? Sailing above the clouds won't happen if you don't take a chance. When it feels right—jump! Take risks. Teach yourself that fear doesn't have a hold of you, lift your chin up, and believe in a positive outcome.

So if something you're pondering feels good and you want to do it, even if you're not sure how, if your heart is calling you to do it, lead with love and do it now. You can figure out the 'how' as you get into it.

I will talk more about this later in my books.

QUESTION: What do I dream about but hold off on doing?

ACTION: 8-week challenge: Newness on the calendar

We often hold off on doing things we dream of because it feels uncomfortable and we don't know how to push our boundaries and explore new things. We allow our attitude of "playing it safe" to dictate our activities and before we know it, life has become a routine that rarely creates waves.

For the next two months, I challenge you to do something new every week. Take your calendar out and choose a specific night. Write a list of eight activities you would like to try and commit to doing one per week. It doesn't have to be big things and can be as small as taking a walk and exploring a new park, or trying a restaurant from a different culture. Just make sure you go a bit out of the ordinary. Be brave, and push your boundaries. If you never try anything new, how can you grow or know if you like it? It's time to start turning the nervous butterflies in your stomach into excited butterflies!

5. Tiny Living—
Challenges of Less

Simplify your Space

"All you need is less." —Carole

How small of a space do you think you need to live and be happy?

Moving aboard a 41 foot long, by 13 1/2 foot wide sailboat was a colossal endeavor. Yes, we'd made the decision, and we were committed to giving life on board a try, but I was 28 and Eric 32 years old at the time, so we were still attached to the get all the toys you can materialistic phase of our lives.

When we bought Windsong, we lived in a three-bedroom house, with two living rooms, a dining room, an efficiency (which our buddy rented), and yes, our personal private bar! It had a coveted outdoor Florida-style living paradise, with a large in-ground swimming pool, complete with water slide, covered patio, and large brick BBQ that could grill for crowds. Even the dog had a condo tiki hut large enough for the kids to play in.

Eric was working at Harley Davidson for three years and had been making a shitload of money, which we spent on discounted Harley stuff. Every inch of the house was decorated with trademark Harley collectibles: alarm clocks, jeans, cutting boards, kitchenware, knick knacks, all the way down to the hangers holding our Harley clothes. We had our beautiful motorcycles parked outside, wore only expensive Harley wear, drank the best, ate the finest, and spent money like it was water. We had achieved what was in our biker days – Harley Heaven. All these toys projected an image of an American dream success story. But we were at an impasse, and at war with how we felt.

It's incredible the amount of stuff that was crammed in our house. When we started the process of downsizing, we first moved from the big house into a small 1-bedroom apartment, located down the street from the Dania Cutoff Canal, where we docked our newly purchased boat. We stayed there for seven months, preparing to transition into a floating life: repainting, rewiring, updating systems, and suiting it for our needs.

It took a lot of guts to let go of all the things we had accumulated and considered treasure at the time. I think what helped is that we had gained all this abundance in such a short amount of time, that we had less fear of letting go. You see, we had done the exact same thing just four years earlier when we emigrated from Canada and downsized a full house into a cargo van which I drove down I-95 to Florida. A few months earlier, my husband rode his motorcycle down there to find work and a place to stay, with everything he could stuff on his Softail.

We were fortunate with a series of events and hard work, which translated into a lot of material things. Still, letting go of all the things we had amassed took some courage because it had been a dream of ours for a long time. Stuff represented stature, security, success, and accomplishment. We came to realize that was just an illusion but we squeezed every ounce of juiciness out of it before embracing that realization.

This lifestyle and all the stuff was weighing us down. It was with a nervous yet hopeful heart that I welcomed the decluttering.

I started the process with major triage:

-What I absolutely could not let go of and would bring on board.

-What I had no attachments to and could be sold.

-What had some emotional attachment but could be "kept in the family" by donating to friends.

-What didn't have much monetary value and would be donated to charity.

-What was too precious or still tugged at the heartstrings was packed and sent to live in my parent's attic in Canada. (Years later, we realized that stuff didn't mean anything to us anymore and it was cluttering their home as well—we asked them to sell it!)

After the initial triage was done, I held my first garage sale and then either sold, gave away, or packed up any remaining items. This was a long time before iPhones, Facebook Marketplace and the various selling apps in use today. What remained after our friends went through everything was packed up in the van, and off I went on a hot sunny day, to hustle my loot for a little bit of gold, at the Swap Shop, a popular flea market in Fort Lauderdale.

It was a huge transformational experience to let go all of these things we had thought for so long were the key to our happiness. Minimalizing was a turning point in my life. Once I got over the initial shock of seeing my belongings walk away in the hands of friends and strangers, I started feeling hopeful instead of empty and stuck. It was still an emotional ride. Let's face it, we are surrounded by a society of consumerism.

We were caught in the big-money-buy-more-stuff lifestyle. Work yourself to the bones to pay for all the toys you can buy, cram all the fancy wares and collectibles into the biggest house you can't afford, drink to excess to hide the stress, and start over in the morning. Eric was burning out, I couldn't keep up, and we weren't happy.

We had lost ourselves in the big house and needed the space of the small boat to find ourselves and put the pieces back together. It was time to simplify our space, redefine what is truly important, and reconnect with each other.

A sailboat has very limited room. First comes the necessary, then comes the practical, and if you have any space left (which for me meant two half shelves and a small ledge), then you can have items out of pure fancy. For that reason, only items that I truly cherished made it on board. The lengthy process was figuring out what things fell into that category.

Then, an unexpected second round of simplifying popped up. The first pile that was supposed to board Windsong had to be sorted through again because it quickly became apparent that I couldn't possibly fit all my favorite things in it. I had to go even further and ask myself, out of all my favorite things, which were the top 20 items that I could not live without? Those items had to be small. Books were rated in the same fashion and I stacked the best of the best in every corner that I could!

For the first six months, I tripped into, bumped against, skinned knees, knocked elbows, jammed fingers, broke nails, and stubbed toes on the angled floors and ledges so many times that swearing and purple bruises were a constant. It was hard to acclimate to the confining space, but I was determined to make it work. We had shelter, food, clothes, and most importantly, we were happy again.

I had to get used to all the nooks and crannies on board. We didn't have a lot of closet space, so we had to get space bags to squish down and seal up our clothes, linens, and supplies. It took a while to organize everything so that it made sense. No space is lost on a boat, there is storage hidden everywhere: under the settee, beds, sofas, behind the backrests of every seat, underneath every step, even part of the counter lifts to store snacks, captain's log, charts, and navigator's instruments. If there was the slightest unused space we quickly converted it into a compartment. That meant that there were so many well-hidden places to put things in that I kept losing stuff! It drove me nuts that I couldn't remember where everything was. We even started an onboard myth that we had gremlins living in the bilge, who liked to come out at night and steal our stuff. A foldable bleacher chair—poof! Gone. Eric's shoe shining kit hasn't been seen since we moved aboard in '97!

And get this, a year after we moved in, we remembered there was a fluorescent light hidden under a skinny wooden ledge in the far corner of the kitchen!

Simplifying our lives was indeed a challenge, but it taught us how amazing making a massive change like this is when you give yourself permission to let go.

Once we started to take Windsong out to sail, we discovered a vast new world of adventures, rich with encounters and memories. Suddenly, we had more freedom and space to live in than we ever could have imagined. Unencumbered by stuff, we were free to explore, free to roam, with more time on our hands to enjoy life and each other's company. It was the best trade-off I'd ever made.

And because I know you're wondering...yes, sharing a small space with another human being (and a dog) also took some adjustments. Such intimate, loving, and close living, is also messy, annoying, frustrating, and teary. It deserves a chapter of its own in a later book.

 LESSON: Simplify your space. Once my mind was decluttered from materialistic attachments, it was free to roam, and expand beyond its horizons. Windsong gave me that. I truly feel that this shift of focus gave me an opportunity to look at the world with new eyes. I had removed myself from the rat race of amassing as many toys as I could before the age of 40—all to unconsciously prove my worth by the accumulation of stuff.

We saw our friends go down the path of large mortgages and expensive cars, and sometimes we did dream about "having it all," but then we'd come home to our cozy little boat, and have the freedom to sail away at a moment's notice, unchained to stuff, and that felt even better.

Our obsessive attachment to material things in our society is at an all-time high. It destroys lives daily. I'm not talking about necessities like clothing and shelter; I'm talking about all the crap we accumulate over the years that has absolutely no use, value, or meaning. Or when we do attach value to it, it's misguided by feelings of lack.

Take for example all the pretty things we had in the house, a treasure to some, and worth a lot of money, but material things just the same. Were these things providing me with love? Inner peace? Confidence? Personal growth? A better relationship? No. They were giving me a false sense of identity and security, and a level of material comfort that was hiding the desolating sense of disenchantment and disconnect in our marriage. Underneath all that stuff, we had been stressed, unhappy, and going on a downhill spiral.

Simplifying our lives allowed us to focus on other things, like our relationship with each other and with ourselves.

Don't get me wrong; I love pretty things! But if something new came on board, it was because it really inspired me. And oftentimes, it meant something else has to go. There is no room for accumulating, so whatever I cherished less, whatever had stopped resonating with me, required my release. So I donated it and allowed my space to stay at its highest vibration. By letting go of the old items that no longer served me, I created space for newer, better things to come into my life that could serve my growth into the better person I was becoming.

Living simply is underrated in our society. Those of us living on this side of that edge are often looked at as obsessive or extremist. I actually feel we are more in touch with nature, the world, and the people surrounding us—the things I've found to truly matter in life.

Simplifying my surroundings helped me stop valuing myself for what I owned on the outside, and start owning up to what was going on inside myself. Free to explore my inner vastness, I found abundance in so many ways.

QUESTION: My house is burning down. I have 5 minutes to save myself and can take three things with me. What are they?

 ACTION: Get rid of clutter

Simplified version: Go in each room of your house (include your closets), and find one thing to release.

Extensive version: Start by simplifying your living space, and only surround yourself with items that fill your heart with absolute joy. Look at all objects in your house that do not have practicality like tools, cooking wear, or safety equipment. Look at all the knick knacks, souvenirs, memorabilia, frames, and decorations. On a scale of 1 to 10, 10 being the highest, only keep the things valued 5 and higher (I'm going easy on you; with Windsong it was 9). Anything lower—get rid of it. Box the items, and place them in your car right away (out of sight, so you don't go back to re-evaluate or commiserate), and donate these items to a shelter.

This exercise will help you see how attached you are to inconsequential things. It's ok to have a comfortable home, but this is an exercise to make you aware of what you focus your energy on, and what you value most. An unhealthy attachment to material things will lead to unhappiness if you take away or lose such things. Do items merit this kind of attachment? How would you handle losing everything?

You cannot make yourself happy by owning things. It's a temporary fix that will keep you locked in a continuous loop of consumerism until you die. You will always want more and more, cluttering your mind with stress over not having, and thinking of ways to acquire, when all you need is to step back, and refocus your mind on what is important in life: relationships, health, honoring our planet, and connecting with people.

Your life will feel more inspired when you create space around your heart to connect deeper with your inner landscape, and creating space in your living room décor is the first step. It's an act of letting go and a declaration to Source that you are open to receive. The benefits you can get from simplifying your space are immense. So declutter today and spread the goods!

6. 911—This is an Emergency

Simplify your Mind

"If you're always on autopilot, you'll miss the journey."
—Carole

My husband is a great worrier. He's always thinking about contingency plans and is a naturally stressed person. His mind is non-stop, from morning to night, Plan A, Plan B, Plan C, "what if's" and possible outcomes. He incessantly thinks about alternatives, and it's also why he's excelled at his job, managing countless employees, turning multiple departments into making profits in the millions. He's always on the lookout for the best way to do things, analyzing, and tallying numbers. Math and numbers and productivity are his forte. But all this constant thinking takes its toll on the mind, body, and spirit. When we decided to move out of the big house into Windsong he ended up in the emergency room from a common American threat.

I'll always remember that day. We were lying on the bed watching TV when he said he wasn't feeling well. We were hungover – again – from a weekend of partying, which was also his attempt to slow the constant thinking. All of the sudden, this strong, larger-than-life, virile man grabbed my arm, with panic in his eyes said he was losing his peripheral vision, that his hands and feet were starting to tingle and he felt pressure on his chest. I could feel my own panic rise when I heard him utter the words, "Call 9-1-1, I think I'm having a heart attack." We were so young! How could that be? I got up to run for the phone but he grabbed my arm and yanked me down. "Don't leave me, I'm starting to see black." We had a roommate and I screamed for her to call 9-1-1, which she did. While we waited, we held hands and he started hyperventilating. I didn't know what to do. This was the first time he ever felt like this. I cried and waited while Eric felt his hands and feet start to curl into his body.

The paramedics arrived, took his vitals and plugged him into all kinds of gages and machines. I had never seen my strong, powerful husband in such a vulnerable way. It was scary. They told him that he was experiencing a full-blown panic attack and that the worst that could happen is that he would fall unconscious, his body would automatically regulate itself, and he would wake up ok. But if he felt he wanted to go to the emergency room to get checked out, he was more than welcome to do so. He needed reassurance so we went, and the doctors confirmed the prognosis. He scheduled a follow up with our primary physician to get medication, and he recommended that Eric make some lifestyle changes to alleviate stress in his life.

For the next six months, Eric experienced regular anxiety attacks, even with the medication they gave him. Some days were better; some days were worse. Once, he drove to the end of our street on his way to work as he had done so often, but this day Eric had to stop and park on the side of 441. As he looked into oncoming traffic, he tried to control the dreaded oncoming panic attack. That day, he turned around and came right back home. The stress was debilitating.

We were waking up to the idea that we are not infallible, and death is always a possibility. When you're young, you think you can go on burning the candle at both ends, forever and ever and life won't catch up to you. It was our first scare and ambulance trip (that wasn't accident-related). Just the thought of losing my husband that day crushed my heart while his was being squeezed.

Eric always felt the need to be on the move, so it was hard for him to go from the habit of living life at 200 miles an hour to a slower pace, especially when he was under pressure and competing on a flat rate scale at work beating time and personal records for money rewards can be highly addictive. Stress causes damage to the body, and the mind emphasizes it with the narrative we tell ourselves.

He needed a pressure valve release, and he needed it fast.

Sailing provided just that. From the first time we set foot on our first boat, I saw an instant transformation. He was breathing life again and genuinely enjoying himself. I loved spending the day out on the water with him, loved watching him relax and become in tune with the boat, the wind, and the waves. Just for a while, his mind calmed and focused on the present moment and the task at hand, raising the sails, finding the perfect angle of the wind for an optimal ride, and tweaking our trajectory to ride the waves. It turned into his own sailing meditation, and while his mind focused on sailing and scanning the horizon for fish and sea life, he let go of his worries.

I've seen it have the same effect on most people who come aboard. There is something about sailing that transcends time and worries. Everyone relaxes into the rhythm of the boat, cradled and carried by the ocean. As if the Great Mother is telling you, "There, there, it will be alright." It has been the provider of great peace in our lives. For myself, being an already pretty relaxed person by nature, this was an opportunity to explore an even deeper layer to quieting the mind.

So if our environment can change our peace of mind so quickly, why do we stay in one that is conducive to stress? No one in their 'right mind' would do that—so you would think, right? I think that we get caught up in the game of life and lose focus on what really deserves our attention. We fill our minds with worry and clutter and stay in it out of habit. And how can an unbalanced mind realize the possibilities of peace when it is overcrowded by endless chaotic thoughts?

I used to worry a lot more about things than I do today. Thanks to our nautical lifestyle, yoga, and meditation, my worry stays at bay. What started as an exercise plan in a gym, ended up changing my life. For me, sailing and yogic philosophies have been the biggest catalysts for transformation. For some, it's the great outdoors, hiking trails, riding bikes, cooking or cleaning. When you can bring your mind entirely into the present moment and truly immerse yourself into your current actions, you let go of regrets about the past or worries about the future. This allows the mind to relax and the inner chatter to quiet.

Sailing just happens to be done in the most beautiful environment that provides a calm and soothing motion. Being surrounded by water is naturally relaxing and comforting, and typically far away from modern noise so you hear only the song of the wind in your sails. It is a winning stress relief combination.

Wherever you find comfort, go to that place, close your eyes, and become present to where you are in your life. Turn off the autopilot and allow your mind to be still—breathe into your essence. Appreciate the moment and focus solely on the now. This is mindfulness; this is being present. The more you do it, the freer your mind will become and the more alive you will feel!

LESSON: Simplify your mind. Sailing has gifted me with the magic of the present moment. Living in gentle movement with nature, at a slower pace than the typical modern life, has helped me unwind and connect with a larger space inside my heart. When I worry, I close off the part of myself which holds solutions to my problems. When I relax, I allow this space to open and activate my creative mind, which in turn soothes my worries, and allows my system to get a much-needed boost. Challenges are not solved by worries; they are solved by inspiration and creative thinking. My mind needs to be free to think outside the box to find solutions and to do so, I must practice mindfulness.

If I want new things in life, I must make room in my house (or boat) for it. If I want new ideas and solutions, I must make room for it in my mind. Carving out time for myself every day to nurture and reconnect with my inner essence will help me problem solve, create possibilities, and stay inspired.

Many practices can bring mindfulness into your life. Whatever method you choose, the number one thing is to do it on a regular basis, every single day. Commit to a daily practice that relaxes the mind. Morning yoga and meditation is my medicine. What's yours?

QUESTION: These are the things that worry me the most...

77

ACTION: 5-4-3-2-1 Technique to help with an anxiety or panic attack

- Make sure you are in a peaceful setting
- Look around you.
- Find 5 separate things you can see and think about them for some time.
- Touch 4 different objects and observe their texture, temperature, and use.
- Listen to 3 distinct sounds and note what makes them resonate and stand out from each other.
- Identify 2 different smells and see if they trigger any memories.
- Get 1 thing you can taste, eat it and observe your taste buds. How does it make you feel? If you don't have food or beverages around, you can taste your fingertip.

This is called grounding and is a great mindfulness exercise. It can help when you feel like you have lost control of your surroundings. Anxiety attacks can be very intense and a person can sometimes feel like they are losing touch with their senses and with reality. Grounding and reconnecting with your body is helpful in many ways.

7. Big Leagues—Sailing the 41 Footer

Simplify Change

"If you want to go somewhere, you'll have to release what anchors you." —Carole

Sailing Windsong was a completely different experience than sailing Wannabe. I would compare it from bicycling on a quiet country road to motorcycling on a fast busy highway. For one thing, I did not have the physical strength to handle the heavy canvas and larger hardware, so I could not raise the sails by myself anymore. So we reversed our roles. I became the helms-woman, and Eric became our rigger and sail master, climbing the lower part of the mast to reach the Mack pack (sail covers), attach the sail to the stay, and raise the sails. It saddened me a bit at first because I loved to raise and be in control of the sails on Wannabe. It was such a thrill to watch the large white triangular sail take a puff of wind and push us onward, knowing that I was the one who lifted it up in the sky. The rush of adrenaline I got when I had to bring them down in a hurry for a spontaneous storm was thrilling. Fortunately, I soon learned to love to navigate and sail our 15-ton sailboat.

There was, of course, a learning curve. We allowed ourselves to test the larger vessel, and how it responded to wind and change. It was so much heavier and slower, but with more grip than anything we'd sailed before. It sliced through the water and parted the seas, balancing its weight on top of a wave and swinging back to climb some more. It was a beautiful thing to feel in control of it while flying on the water. It took some time to adapt, but we learned to be flexible and became a great team.

One of the first times that I remember getting high on sailing, was on Biscayne Bay one hot afternoon. Eric was downstairs in the motor room fixing something and I was sailing Windsong, completely in charge and in tune with the boat. The wind was perfect—I was immersed in tweaking the boat as I drove topless (this was Miami after all), tanned like an island girl, smoking a cigar (yes, I used to smoke). I tightened and pushed at the right angle, then released the helm just long enough on the crease of the wave, playing with the wind and currents to squeeze every knot I could to get Windsong to go as fast as possible. I got so excited, and completely forgot that Eric was downstairs, head upside down, doing repair work when I screamed, "HONEY!!! I'm freaking doing 7.5 knots!" This was almost Windsong's maximum speed.

He popped his head in the companionway, to see his half-naked wife with the biggest grin on her face, puffing away like a kingpin. He told me later he felt a wave of pride wash over him, before he said, "Just remember your husband downstairs trying to fix the motor with his ass over his head!"

He knew then, I could handle the boat, and he could count on me in an emergency.

One such time came a few years later when we needed to dock Windsong under sail in a challenging 20-knot wind. Usually, we would turn the motor on to sail through the narrow channel leading us from the ocean to our lagoon and marina, and we always used the reverse to stop the boat from moving forward, but that weekend we ran into trouble. The elbow of the exhaust was clogged and started sending smoke throughout the boat, raising panic and the fire alarms. Our engine had overheated so we couldn't use it. It wasn't drastic but it meant we were completely under sail-only power to dock the boat.

Our longtime friend Big Pete from Quebec was on board and needed
to come to shore so he could catch a plane home. I would have to move
fast enough to get into the slip and have complete control over the 15-
ton vessel so it would not drift sideways and crash onto our neighboring
boats. The guys were in charge of tying spring lines from the boat to the
pilling as soon we sailed past them with no seconds to spare, in order to
stop the boat from crashing into the cement wall at the end of the slip.
That was the, "tour de force."

A moving mass on the water doesn't stop on a dime and will keep on
moving until there's friction or drag (Newton's First Law), and we didn't
have a motor with reverse to act as the resisting force that day. Breaking
its momentum would be up to tying the beast in its stall and holding on
with all their might.

I remember the first year we got Windsong; I practiced for days
throwing dock lines from the pier trying to grab stationary pilings
lasso-style just a few feet away from me. Easier said than done! This
was one of my duties every time we docked the big boat. I can't say
how many times the lines ended up in the water missing their target, but
we normally had the motor on to help steer back and forth in the slip.
Playing cowboy with a rope is a lot harder than it looks and this day the
pressure was on the boys to not miss so we wouldn't completely destroy
the bow of our boat.

I was in control of the helm. Ouf! What a gut-wrenching experience
this was. I felt so much pressure! My palms were sweaty and my heart
was drumming a solo. Thank goodness there was a small lagoon where
we could turn around, get prepared, and get in gear. I lined up the vessel
with our destination slip and went for it. (A slip is like a parking spot
where you "park" or berth your boat, usually between 4 pilings by a
pier). Eric was guiding me. It was not an easy task to keep Windsong
straight in such wind at slow speed. All it wanted to do was what it was
built for; use that wind to speed up and sail away, the exact opposite of
what we wanted. It was like trying to keep a racing horse calm in its stall

after it hears the bell ring. The slip was only 14 feet wide, and our beam is 13.5. You read that right—we were docking in the tightest slip we'd ever been in, with barely three inches to spare on either side. But that's why we have rub rails right?

It took some lining up in order to not ram the boats next to us. Friendly neighbors were coming out to welcome us back home, and could tell something was off. Through guts and sailing skills, we sailed towards our slip, and just at the last moment, when Eric knew we would glide in our slip without fail, he dropped the sail while I aimed it straight. But we were coming in fast, so the guys positioned themselves on each side, and as soon as we were close enough, they threw the spring lines over the pilings, tied them down as tight as they could, and physically threw themselves on the pilings, holding on as tight as they could to stop us from crashing into the cement seawall. Without a motor, there was no reverse on Windsong so their strength, and the lines, were the only thing stopping the boat from crashing at ramming speed into the wall and causing thousands of dollars of damage (and maybe an unexpected new porthole window view in Big Pete's bedroom)!

The lines stretched, the men growled, and the boat stopped. We made it. Windsong was docked barely a foot away from the seawall. The neighbors applauded, and everyone told me what a great sailor I had become. It was a proud moment in my life. I was grateful that I had my big Viking by my side, and my towering friend to bounce off our landing.

Big Pete now had another exciting story to tell our Canadian friends back home; the day we parked a 15-ton boat with mere skill and human strength.

R.I.P. Big Pete, we love you.

LESSON: Simplify change. I'm glad I embraced change and learned a new role in steering the big boat. Sometimes it can be scary to jump into a different position when things are changing, and everything is new. We often make a big case against it and tell ourselves all kinds of stories why we don't like change. We dread, resist, and do everything in our power to keep change from happening. But what happens if we broaden our perspective and welcome change into our lives?

If we simplify the process and take it one step at a time we can learn to embrace it. Change is an opportunity for us to bring more awareness into our life. It breaks the routine and offers us new ways of seeing and doing things. It opens doors of new possibilities. It's an opportunity for us to shift our conversation and perspective.

What if, when faced with change, you would have this conversation:

"There is a change in my life. It's taking me outside of my comfort zone. My routine has changed and it affects things I was used to doing a certain way. It feels different. It brings up insecurities I have. I am not sure yet whether I like it or not. I may need to learn new skills in order to adapt. This is not how I had imagined my life. I am willing to have an open mind and embrace the process. Change is here to support my evolution. It can bring me great joy and needed life lessons. This may push my limitations but I will love and respect myself while I take time to transition into his new phase in my life. I am not alone. Others have had to deal with changes like this. There are people and places that can help me with this. I am strong and resilient and will thrive through this change. I am supported by life's ever changing ways."

Have compassion by allowing yourself the time and space to adapt to new things without judging yourself too harshly. Be mindful of your inner chatter and practice self-love. The more you embrace change, the easier it will become and the more confidence you will have facing new challenges.

Change is part of life, we cannot grow (or even live) without it. We all have our own way of transitioning so do what feels right for you but don't baby yourself. Look for the silver lining. There is light behind every cloud. Change is just a new way to be! And, remember, change today may mean saving the day (or at least the bow of your own proverbial boat) tomorrow!

QUESTION: What is the one thing in my life I wish I could change?

 ACTION: Role Reversals

If you have a partner, ask them to reverse roles in the house for a week. If you are the chef, you are now on laundry duty or balancing the checkbook, and vice versa. If you live by yourself, change your routine. Go out on a weeknight, invite a friend over to play a game, try a new restaurant. Even the slightest habit changes (like switching the hand you typically use to hold your toothbrush) opens up and strengthens your brain, and your will. Continue adding another small change, and another and pretty soon, you start to look forward finding new ways to go through life. Simplifying change, helps you master change. In a world like this one, that's a valuable skill, no doubt!

8. Ocean Crossing—a Whole New World

Simplify your Obstacles

"In sailing, as in life, timing is everything." —Carole

7/21/1998. First Mate's Log.

DAY ONE. Dinner Key. Be prepared. On the water, anything can happen or hit you at any time.

It was the first time we were going to sail across the "big" ocean, a 48 nautical mile crossing from Florida to the island chain of the Bahamas. It may not sound far, but it would be the first time we would lose sight of land and be completely isolated on the open sea. Until that day, we had been coastal sailors, always just a few miles of shore, gradually learning the art of sailing, and dipping our toes into the deeper waters. There is a vast difference between coastal sailing and offshore sailing; one is done in the safety of being close to land and just a quick radio call away from a Coast Guard rescue, the other, you're on your own, miles away and out of sight from land. You have no landmark to help you navigate, and must rely on your accurate calculations between wind, currents, drift, and sailing speed, to navigate to your destination. A few degrees off, and you can miss your target by miles, and end up lost in the big blue sea. Nowadays, with GPS and chart plotters, even the greenest of sailors can venture out to the big beyond. When we got into sailing, the country was just starting to phase out the old LORAN-C navigation system for the new Global Positioning System. GPS precision was still inaccurate and off by miles, intentionally blurred by the military for security reasons.

So in the early days of GPS navigating, you still had to rely on paper charts, calculations, and your own wits.

Can you imagine finding yourself with hundreds of feet of water under your feet, and no stable land in sight? Miles and miles of ocean swaying and moving around you, nothing stable around you except the horizon, a sea of fluidity with all kinds of sea creatures living in it–some happy to chomp on you for breakfast. The only person in charge of your safety is you and in my case, my husband. This was the late 90s; there were no iPhones or cell reception out there. We were completely on your own.

It's a strange feeling; at the same time exhilarating and petrifying. We felt very small, and no matter how prepared we were, or how many navigating courses we took, it's one of those big moments in life we will always remember. We were planning on crossing the ocean the following morning.

Our good friends Gina and Jean-Pierre had flown in for the occasion. It was the first time on a sailboat for the French couple. They were eager to help and excited about the trip.

The boat was loaded to capacity with five weeks' worth of food for four people, drinks, snacks, beer, and wine. We were heavy with fuel and water and had enough of everything to sink the ship and send everyone to rehab (I was still drinking at this point).

We had plotted our course to cross over to Bimini, Bahamas, from Miami's Biscayne Bay, about 25 miles south of where we were docked in Hollywood. It was a more strategic angle for our boat to surf the Gulf Stream current and ride the southern winds north east to Bimini. So we needed to sail south first in order to go north-east and then cross.

The Gulf Stream is an offshore prevailing current, moving south to north between the landmasses. It's like a 30-mile wide river inside the ocean running about 2-3 knots, sometimes faster, so you don't want to meet it head-on because it will make for a very difficult and wet ride, and will slow you down tremendously. If you position your boat correctly, you can take advantage of the direction of the current to propel you even faster to your destination and surf across the ocean, enjoying a more comfortable ride.

Since a tropical wave was over us, the weather on the ocean was terrible. The nine-foot seas were too large for us to cross, so we had to wait for a weather window to open. Thankfully, with the Intracoastal available to us, it meant that we could still make our way south using the tourist route, sailing down the waterway all day, and see South Florida's best neighborhoods from the water. (The Intracoastal is a 3,000-mile inland waterway that runs from Boston to the southern tip of Florida, made up of natural inlets, saltwater rivers, bays and sounds, and man-made artificial canals.)

We raised many levy bridges, sailed by inlets, drooled over luxurious neighborhoods with countless mansions, encountered tons of boats of all kinds, and saw Miami downtown and its landmarks from up close. We sailed through the Port of Miami, and finally reached our anchorage for the night: the protected waters of Biscayne Bay.

It was a great trip and showed our friends just how beautiful South Florida is from the water. The traffic is very hectic, with speed boats (yes, just like Miami Vice!), cruise ships, fishing boats, water taxis, pleasure boats, bridges to open, canoes, paddleboards, islands and sandbars to avoid. It's a fun tour, but you have to be extra vigilant for Miamians out on the water, enjoying their favorite leisure time.

On top of that, our nervous excitement for our upcoming crossing was tangible. Throughout the day, Eric had given everyone the safety guidelines, and went over onboard emergency procedures, as we casually motored down the waterway.

By dinner time, we were anchored in a popular anchorage with a view of the Miami skyline, scarfing down an amazing meal. We'd wanted to cross at dawn, but it looked like the oceans were still too messy for safe passage. We would have to keep listening to the weather station and stay put until the winds and seas subsided. It was amazing to be out on the Bay, but we were so prepared and ready, and just wanted to cross the ocean already! We crashed into bed, tired and jolly, and eager for our big trip.

I was roused from my sleep as quite suddenly, our boat was traveling very fast towards the right side and heeling dangerously. Holy Shit! My head was jerked lower than my feet, and everything shook and moved. We were heeling 15 degrees to starboard, and Windsong was laying down under an oncoming gale-force wind, which pushed it to the end of its anchor chain. We jerked violently, stopped for a second, then started to veer towards the other side, swung to the left and jerked hard again. We were bare pole sailing (no sails up) at anchor and for a heavy Morgan to do so, it was a damn bad sign.

We bolted out of bed and scrambled upstairs. Our boat has two companionways (entryways to lower level), one ladder goes down to the master stateroom (our bedroom), and the other goes to the front of the boat, separating us from the galley (kitchen), salon area, and forward berth (front bedroom) where our guests slept. There is a passageway inside connecting forward and aft (front and rear).

When the squall hit and leaned the boat, it woke everybody up. We all ran in a panic up the ladders to see what the heck was going on. Eric and I jumped up the ladder as fast as we could, eyes wide and completely naked, and JP ran up the fore ladder in front of us. He told us later that we were quite the sight to see!

Outside mayhem reigned. Before dinner we swam and snorkeled around the boat and hadn't put away our stuff. We were air drying bathing suits, towels, noodles, water toys, and gear was everywhere.

Everything lightweight was airborne, and a lot of it lost. Cushions and noodles flew overboard; a towel was drifting and sinking away.

We were in the middle of a feisty rogue storm pouring buckets on us. It was howling so loud, with winds of over fifty miles per hour. A neighboring boat had his wind generator on, and the blades got caught up in the oncoming force of the wind, screaming a high pitched sound of screeching metal against the force of nature. We could see the boater outside on his boat between squalls of rain, but it was too dangerous at this speed to try anything. He would have to pray that it holds, and steer clear of it until then.

Our bimini top was secured by straps and snaps, and the wind was so strong that it started unsnapping them and the Strataglass, sending the windows flying. My goodness, it was going to tear the windows off and take the bimini with the wind! It was a crazy gale storm. Eric turned the motor on and put it in gear, in case we'd start to drag anchor, then ran outside with JP to try salvaging our belongings, and secure what they could.

I grabbed the bottom of the windows and held on. Windsong was slamming into the waves and wind. Boats in the anchorage were jerking around their chains, and we could see other boaters out trying to secure their vessels. The guys dragged our heavy dive gear bag on top of the bottom of the windows and saved our bimini enclosure.

Our captain was still in his 'birthday suit' while piercing rain hammered his ass in this torrential downpour, he was a funny sight to see when he finally jumped back in the cockpit!

The unattended sailboat in front of us suddenly lost its anchor and flew right by us, barely missing Windsong, and slammed into the houseboat anchored behind us. Its captain frantically ran outside, trying to fend it off, but the force of the storm was too high, so he ended up tying it rafted to his boat — both riding out the storm on the same anchor.

Our boat was sailing around its anchor from left to right, trying to untie itself like a wild horse in a fury. We were lucky; our anchor was well set. After putting some clothes on we spent the rest of the storm in the cockpit, which didn't last long, hiding behind the windows and holding them in place.

We could hear TowBoatUs calling on the VHF radio on working channel 16. He was very pissed off at being caught in this in an opened cockpit vessel, a few miles offshore, with no warning from the weather channel. He was so mad and warned other boats of the incoming gale. Poor guy. We turned to the weather channel, and they were still announcing: "calm breeze, calm seas, and clear skies." It was the twilight zone. Typically, the Coast Guard weather stations are pretty accurate in their forecasts. It is, after all, imperative to the safety of boaters. This one went unclaimed and undetected.

When the sky cleared, it was evident that many boats had done some major shuffling, dragging anchors or completely losing them. Two had ended up on the beach, and one was well-grounded in shallow waters. We were lucky to avoid a collision with an escaped vessel. There was a lot of debris floating around, and the water remained choppy the rest of the night. Mother Nature is not a force to mess around with. She does as she pleases, and goes where and when she wants. That storm sealed the deal on the need to be prepared, have a plan, and always, always put away your stuff before going to bed!

DAY TWO. When the path is clear: GO

Knowing that we still could not cross that day, we slept in late the following morning and lounged around, recuperating from our overnight adventure. Today was not the day that we could cross to the Bahamas, but maybe tomorrow. The first thing we always do when we wake up is to listen to the weather station to assess our day. A good day out on the water is measured by the quality of the weather. They were calling for a weather window to open the following day, so we planned on leaving early at dawn, and finally earn our ocean crossing badge. We would only have this chance to cross because high seas were coming back the next few days. Sailors often play a game of cat and mouse with weather systems, it's never a good idea to get caught in them, and best to avoid the temptation of crossing when danger is announced, no matter how eager you are to go.

This wait was only making us more tense like a kid on Christmas morning finding out he can't open his presents just yet.

After the guys spent the morning rescuing a young woman whose boat had dragged and ran aground on the flats in the overnight storm, Eric decided to bring us to an anchorage closer to the inlet so that we could simply round the peninsula at dawn and be out to sea. This was the same peninsula where we'd had our butts kicked, a little over a year ago on Wannabe. It was a few hours trek to cross the bay, and it was a perfect day. It was summertime, and the sun was hot. Boatloads (literally) of Miamians were out on the water, enjoying their favorite pastime. This extra day out on the boat before crossing would help Gina and JP acclimate to the motion of the boat, and help them get their sea legs. We sunbathed and sailed, while Eric, taught JP how to tweak the sails to get the most speed out of Windsong. We were blessed with dolphin sightings—an omen for a good trip. I felt positive about the next day.

We got to the new anchorage and Eric started the BBQ for dinner, as we took turns taking our showers on deck before the sun went down. We didn't have a hot water heater back then, so we used a sun shower, a small bladder that uses the sun to warm the water. You also had the option of taking a room temperature shower inside. It didn't really matter since we lived in a tropical climate, and the room temperature was never very cold, but slightly cool to the skin. It was a bit frisky at night though. It took us five years to install a water heater on board. I boiled water for dishes; we had the sun shower outside and took our showers in the marinas when we docked.

Everyone thought we were going to have a good night's sleep. We were slumbering in our sweats in the cockpits, while Eric had been listening to the weather channel on the radio. There was a window right now. The system had moved faster than expected, and by mid-morning, the seas would start building up again. We needed eight hours to cross. If we didn't cross overnight, we would lose our chance to visit the Bahamas while our friends were in the US. The path was clear, we had to do it. Time to commit. Our first crossing on the ocean would have to be at night? Well, that was unexpected.

As you probably can tell by now, I'd gotten used to unexpected adventures with Captain Fontaine. He was so excited; there was no way he was going to sleep. We raised the anchor, and off we went into the falling sunset.

It was an enormous feeling to know that soon we would be surrounded by the biggest mass of water we've ever been on and lose sight of land for hours on end, AND we would do it in the dark of night. Anything could happen, and a small mishap at sea can turn deadly quickly. We had to be vigilant and on watch at all times. Crossing at night would cut our visibility to almost null. We didn't have radar and plotted our course by sight, charts, calculations, and late nineties imprecise GPS coordinate. It was petrifying and at the same time exhilarating. But it felt right, so we sailed out to sea. As the sunset behind the Miami coast, Windsong and its crew disappeared into the night.

LESSON: Simplify your obstacles. Obstacles can quickly turn into dangerous hazards if you don't identify them quickly and clear them from your path. Once you know what you want and where you want to go, you must also assess the best way to attain your goal without causing harm or losing your grit.

Many precious lives have been lost in history due to the unwillingness of people to admit when they are out of their league. We weren't ready for an ocean crossing. We weren't even prepared for an unexpected storm at anchor! Simplifying our obstacles meant that the crew identified the problem, took quick actions to secure the boat, and learned what to do in an emergency.

We also had a whipping reminder of simplifying our space before moving on to our next goal!

Our greenhorn team kept their eyes focused on our goal and handled everything that blocked our way right away and without delay. There's always a steep learning curve when you start something new but obstacles are opportunities to grow and learn.

Challenges and unexpected events can be handled with ease and grace by admitting when you are stuck and face an obstacle. Start by taking any steps that are in your power to accomplish right now. Move on to larger hurdles once you've done all that you can to lift your sails. Surround yourself with a crew willing to go the extra mile and don't be afraid to ask for help!

The key to dancing with obstacles is being flexible, swirl if you must, and adapt to whatever life throws at you.

QUESTION: What obstacle(s) stand in the way of my goals and dreams?

 ACTION: Labyrinth

Walking a labyrinth is an age-old form of meditation practiced by many different faiths for spiritual quest, contemplation, or prayer. Walking or even building a labyrinth can be extremely introspective. It is a metaphor for life's journey.

I've had a few experiences in my life when I felt lost, and walking a labyrinth brought me answers. More than a few times, I've felt tremendous relief and gratitude for the simple journey of walking a path towards the center, pausing in deep silence, and walking back out with new found peace, and clear actions to take toward whatever obstacles I was facing. I'm so grateful for my friend Marianne who introduced me to the magic of labyrinth! It has helped me to clarify my thoughts and simplify my path.

To find a labyrinth in your area, check out the website: labyrinthlocator.com

When you get there, stand in front of the entrance of the labyrinth and center yourself by taking a few breaths. Acknowledge yourself for being there and for being open to walking the path and receiving whatever guidance comes to you. Walk the serpentine path in silence, deliberately putting your mind on your footsteps. Be observant of the thoughts, questions, and feelings that arise. When you have reached the center, take a few minutes to pause and reflect. Walk slowly back out. Journal about your experience as you may wish to revisit the wisdom of your walk.

9. Landfall Ahead—
Welcome to the Bahamas

Simplify your Dreams

"Constant adjustments are needed for an optimal course to your dreams." —Carole

We felt immense trepidation at making our first ocean crossing. At the time, it was our Mount Everest and one of the most extreme things we had done.

As we sailed away from shore, we not only lost sight of the South Florida coast, but we lost sight of everything else around us as the night grew dark. Blackness and vastness of water enveloped us and hid us from the rest of the world. Suddenly we became insignificant, a speck in a sea that covers 75% of the world. Virgins of the ocean, it was exhilarating not to know what to expect and find ourselves on a larger scale of life.

Under the cover of night, and sailing the tip of the Bermuda Triangle, we could disappear and be lost at sea with no one ever knowing what became of us. It was quite the feeling, but as green as we were, we had youth's confidence and exuberance, and although a bit on edge, the overall atmosphere on Windsong was nervous positivity.

So as we embarked on this grand adventure, our only challenge was figuring out the directions of the lights coming at us from distant ships sailing at sea, and making sure we stayed out of their way. It was a much harder task than expected and provided hours of entertainment. You'd be surprised at the amount of cargo ships out on the shipping lanes at night.

We sailed under a canopy of stars until the moon came up and covered us with glistening blue-grey light. Incredible to think people used to go around the world in rafts made of wood without any modern comforts and be at sea for months on end – what adventurous souls they were!

It was in this enthralling foreign element that we first started talking about chartering. That night, the magic was real. We were doing it. We bought the boat of our dreams and were sailing to a different country. Where could we go next? This boat could travel the world. Could we? Windsong opened our eyes to the possibilities of living life on a much larger scale than we'd allowed ourselves to dream. I think this was one of the first times that I broke free from the box that defined my life. Attending art school in Montreal for a small town girl really changed my perception of what I thought my life would be. Buying my first motorcycle as a single young woman in college in the 80's was definitely a trailblazing move. Then moving from Canada to Florida, USA was a big thing, but we were still on land with similar lives; we saw it as a zip code change. Now we had completely changed our entire lifestyle. Here we were, four troubadours, Eric and I with basic knowledge including a Coast Guard navigations class, and our guests; two greenhorns full of courage and eager to take on the ocean with us!

Hours went by and our nerves settled. We felt like real sailors now. Explorers of the seas! What a personal accomplishment! We settled into the rhythmic cadence of the boat, and after a few hours Gina and I went below to get a few hours of sleep so we could start taking shifts. In the dead of night, Eric woke me up, and we switched crew so the captain could rest his eyes before we entered Bahamian waters. Then at the break of dawn, a spectacular sun rose in front of us, and we could see a tiny speck on the horizon. By the time we sailed closer to the island of Bimini, the change of ocean color was obvious and utterly different than what we left behind. The murky opaque grey waters turned into clean, transparent turquoise with deep vibrant blues.

Everyone was up for this occasion, nervous and alert, and stunned by the view of palm trees and sandy beaches waiting for us. We had a cruising guide, which told us that we had to find and align two red posts on the beach, which acted as a range and marked the entrance of the channel. As we got closer and closer, the transparent water played tricks on us and fooled us into thinking that we had no depth and were going to run aground, but we were simply navigating unpolluted waters! It was clear water like we'd never before. You could see seashells and starfish at the bottom of the ocean in 10 feet of water!

It was unsettling because it looked like at any minute we would slam the sandy bottom, but we made our way slowly and found the range. The channel had us come so close to the beach that we could have jumped in and swam easily to shore. It was postcard-perfect with a few islanders walking on the beach. We had reached paradise. It felt amazing to be able to do this on our own, in our own home and be able to share this with our friends.

The following weeks were idyllic. We cruised, swam, visited islands, ate fabulous meals, and had the times of our lives. It was the first of many amazing trips. What a blessed way to live! Could we do this all the time? Many before us had done it, they left everything behind and sailed away… and got paid to live their dream… but was it ours?

When we initially bought the boat, we had visions of sailing around the world and chartering Windsong to help us to do that. Simply put, we'd get paid to take people on vacation around the world. We devoured every book on sailing, boating, navigating, offshore cruising, provisioning, first aid, maintenance, and chartering. We subscribed to every boating magazine and drilled every cruiser we met with a barrage of questions.

Each weekend, we'd take Windsong out and improve our sailing skills. We'd cruise down to Biscayne Bay, and spend the weekend sailing and conducting drills. Every holiday was an excuse for an extra-long trip. We'd cram a bunch of friends on board, sail all day to a destination, and meet up with other boater friends for the weekend. We'd tie all the boats together, creating floating rafts of 4-5 boats, and party all night. Those were the days.

The only thing is, being captain and owners of the boat gave us the responsibility of looking out for people and making sure everyone was safe. We found ourselves becoming babysitters, continually reminding people of dangerous onboard situations, and picking up after them. An accident happens so quickly, and on the water, you can't dial 911 and expect rescue to show up in 5 minutes.

It was an awkward position. We were used to being the party-goers, not the supervisors. If managing our friends was proving to be this difficult, we realized it would be harder to tame down paying customers.

Our biggest wakeup call was when we spent a weekend at "Beer Can Island" – the name clues you in that it's a famous boater's party spot on a small island on the Intracoastal close to Miami. It's located by the Sunny Isle inlet famous for its flat, shallow water where small crafts can beach their boat on the sandy bottom, swim, and hang in the water for the day, it even has a floating cantina boat selling hot dogs and hamburgers. It's usually a bustling area with fishermen, boaters, and travelers all vying for space, and trying to sail inside the tightly marked channels to avoid running aground on the shifting sandbar.

We had rafted up in the deeper end of the cove by Big Sandspur (aka Beer Can Island), with four other boats for a weekend of sun and fun. We had powerboats and sailboats, dinghies, water toys, floaters, boaters, bikers, friends from all walks of life, and a lot of refreshments.

Trying to keep a rowdy crew of 20 young adults, who were drinking, bikini-baking in the hot Florida sun, skinny dipping, snorkeling, and just being happy, silly people from doing what they're doing is like trying to train 20 puppies to sit and stay at the same time.

We issued so many warnings of "please don't sit on my couch with your salty wet bathing suit," or "please don't' walk downstairs on my new carpet with sand on your feet," or "please don't throw anything in the toilet unless it has gone through you first."

One friend brought his new girlfriend for the trip, and she had a few too many libations. She was a cigarette smoker. Throughout the day, I repeatedly asked her to smoke on the stern (back) of the boat, and for the umpteenth time, she ended up smoking on the bow (front) of the boat. Since a boat is always anchored with nose to the wind, the ashes of her cigarettes were blowing behind her. Not only were the ashes scattered across the white fiberglass, but one landed on our sunbathing cushions. You guessed it—it caught fire.

She was still talking and smoking away when I screamed at the top of my lungs, "FIRE!!!" and ran to grab the cushion and throw it overboard. In a matter of seconds, the one little cigarette ash burned a 12-inch hole in that cushion. We were so lucky because the hatches were opened, which means the cushion could have easily landed below without anyone being alerted before it was too late.

That was the straw that broke the camel's back. We realized if our friends acted this way (they meant no harm, but were there to cut loose, not pay attention), then how could we manage life on board with complete strangers for weeks at a time? These would likely be people who felt they "owned" the right to do what they pleased on Windsong (our home) because they paid good money for their sailing vacation. We'd heard some horror stories about this from friends who had chartered, and honestly, we were not the most gracious hosts when it came to protecting our home and inner sanctum. This scenario wasn't aligned with who we were and how we truly wanted to live our lives.

Our early years of sailing represented a period of transition. We were still partying hard and finding our way into a different lifestyle, learning a new way of being, discovering what we liked and didn't like, and adjusting to living together in a confined space. We dreamed big dreams and sometimes found those dreams (or elements of those dreams) were not realistic or aligned with who we were becoming.

Chartering is a fantastic way to see the world if you're the right kind of people who can take on the responsibility with ease and flexibility. We couldn't treat Windsong as a working boat, this was our home, and we wanted people to respect it as such. To most, it was a big water toy. When living in a small enclosed space, in a vast sea of unknown—everything is magnified. You have to think of every detail, like where to put your stuff so that it doesn't roll out and trip someone causing an injury and where to place important things for quickest access in case of emergency. Then there's the details of where to stow away all passports, flashlights, a knife to cut lines, the emergency radio, the abandon-ship overboard ditch bag, etc. Oh, and, where to sit, where to walk, when to walk, what to hold on to for support, what's dangerous, what to do, what not to do. On a boat constant vigilance is imperative, or you can bet something will happen.

We got very clear that this was a bigger game than we initially expected. It takes special kinds of people to charter a boat, and we weren't ready to pay the potential price to do it. So we simplified our vision and became full-time liveaboards instead. A crew of two, plus our dog, with the occasional well-vetted guests and close friends. That was a simple solution we could live with, because it aligned with our nature.

LESSON: Simplify your dreams. Which visions or ideals are you holding onto that might have reached their expiration date? Is it may be time to let go? Are the signs telling you it's time to move on but you refuse to reframe your vision? Some dreams aren't meant to be completed. Instead, the purpose is to help us temporarily align our energies to a goal as we move through life and discover a better, higher path.

Our chartering dream pushed us to learn all that we could about living aboard and sailing, to gain the knowledge we needed to be more proficient sailors. It helped us realize that we didn't have to limit our dreams to small things, we could dream as big as the world. It helped us observe our relationship with people around us from a completely new perspective, and look at our wants and needs under a different light. It made us more aware of what we wanted to bring into our lives, and what we could live without.

When you see signs of resistance in your life in the way of bumps on the road, or something always going wrong with your project, that confirms that the energy isn't flowing. Reassess what you are trying to accomplish.

Accidents are a great telltale sign. Another sign is when you find yourself in similar situations over and over again, then you know something needs to change. You are not in alignment, and it's time to simplify the dream you're in. Don't be attached to the outcome. Learn to let go of projects or goals if it doesn't satisfy you anymore. It's okay to refocus your energy into something else even when this goal was a big part of your life for a long time. We all change, our dreams are meant to change right along with us.

If you are uncertain about what you want in life, simplify your quest to: "What do you love? and "What do you dislike?"

Remember, what you resist, persist. So if you're bumping your sails against strong winds, it may be that the Universe is trying to show you a better way. Explore how it feels to be in the flow by saying "Yes!" to things you like to do.

QUESTION: What's missing in my life?

 ACTION: Local Library and Community College

This one is to help you step up your game from our eight-week newness challenge in chapter four. Check out your local library and community college for classes that may pique your interest. For example, one year I decided that if I was to live in South Florida I would like to learn to speak Spanish, so I went to my local high school for special education classes and took a beginner's intro to Spanish. I loved it so much I continued on to my community college for a level 2 Spanish class. It was just a step towards getting me out of the house and trying new things to get me closer to figuring out what I wanted in life. Sometimes we're stuck; unsure of which directions to take, it's not always about the exact waypoint you're set to but the mere fact that you are moving forward that will give you momentum. The more you try things, the more awakened to your dreams you will become. Plus, you will develop the confidence to try things by yourself and meet new people while doing it.

10. Real Sailors— Shenanigans on Paper

Simplify your Schedule

"In the end, we only regret the chances we didn't take."
—*Carole*

Cocktail hour can generate a lot of laughs, but also a lot of great ideas… sometimes.

It was customary to get together every day on the dock and talk about our day or the latest gossip from around the marina. We had a very lively group in those early years, and our dock parties were considered the funniest gatherings in the Fort Lauderdale area. Our group included retired military, world cruisers, airplane mechanics, engineers, nurses, telecommunications experts, self-made millionaires, truckers, old 60's hippies, artists, bikers, and bums. We had a wide range of opinions and life history, but we all agreed on one thing: living aboard was the best life.

And we all agreed that there were a lot of people out on the water who didn't belong at the helm.

There was a playful rivalry between power boaters and sailors sitting at the table, who teasingly called each other "stink potters" and "rag boaters." Or worse, "WAFY" for Wind Assisted F&%king Idiots. It was all in good fun, but you can imagine the colorful conversations!

Most of the boating literature on the market is directed at yachters and sailing clubs, and we had difficulty identifying with that. We lived and breathed sailing, read everything we could put our hands on, took the Coast Guard auxiliary courses, and boating was part of our everyday life, but what we saw on the waters rarely reflected what was portrayed in the glossy fancy magazines.

The stories heard on our docks and things we witnessed were so freaking hilarious, outrageous or ridiculous, that one day, my husband jokingly said, "We should start a magazine and publish all these stories." There was a moment of silence; then, everyone turned to look at me; the graphic designer who knew how to do that, and broke out in smiles and encouraging cheers. This is how Real Sailors Magazine was born. Partly a joke, partially a challenge, it would take on a life of its own.

Scared, nervous, and exhilarated at the same time, I went to talk to a friend who published a motorcycle magazine and asked a lot of questions. With encouragement, he introduced me to his printer. It took me a few months to start the company, design the magazine, and rally some support from advertisers to launch our first issue. It was a very proud moment in my life. Real Sailors was published bi-monthly at 20,000 copies, from West Palm Beach, all the way down to Key West. It was a complimentary magazine found in marina, boater's hangouts, cruising cafés, and marine stores. We had columns on diving, fishing, sailing, tips, had a centerfold – a sailorette of the month – and everything was created to make you laugh, including our very own Viking mascot cartoon adventures.

We were all about poking through the manicured image of yachties and adding some freedom and cheers back into the sport. It didn't take long, and we had a dedicated fan base eager to follow us at dinghy* runs and regatta events in Florida and the Bahamas.
(*a dinghy is a small boat, often carried on board or towed and used as a lifeboat or tender to a larger vessel.)

For a graphic designer like me, it was a dream come true to publish my very own magazine and be my own boss. It was my first take at being an independent entrepreneur, and I loved it. I had a small team of sales reps, writers, and a webmaster to bring it to life. My sidekick and favorite liveaboard neighbor was Bob. He and I were given press passes to all the boat races and boat shows were invited to speak at yacht club events, and mingle with the movers and shakers in the South Florida Marine Industry.

I had the opportunity to go on the Coast Guard base and interview servicemen in the command center. I went to the port to interview pilots and tried the million-dollar simulators at the high tech marine colleges. I met so many folks from all kinds of backgrounds, each with one common passion: boating.

We organized dinghy runs, which were an annual highlight of many people's year and planned mega fun regattas to the Bahamas. Life was a constant flurry of activities and parties and at first it was amazing. We were living the life. I was proud and delighted that I had acted on an idea, and went out there and did it. But the second year, it became a chore. I spent more time on the boat behind a computer while everyone else was enjoying themselves. I was always working. When I was having fun, it was part of working. After the events or parties, I was back at the computer editing photos and writing articles late into the night. And when the end of the month came with the print deadline fast approaching, my week turned into a frenzy, with midnight edits, last-minute customer changes on ads, and a scramble to get everything off to the printer in time for the first of the month publishing. It became a ball and chain, and I was drowning in work.

Tragically, September 11, 2001, happened. Like everyone else, I spent the following days crying and in shock. For months after the towers came down, the country stopped breathing. Everything was in limbo, and the unknown future scared everyone. "Will we go to war? What will happen next? Will it happen again?" While the country went into mourning, and fear gripped the world, the shockwave hit the economy bad. All advertising stopped, and our pockets ran dry. It took miracles at juggling bills to keep the magazine afloat while paying for our expenses out of our personal credit cards, and the printing costs were killing us.

We had to come to the conclusion months later that since we were still not profitable and were never fully able to recover from that hit, we could not repay the debts incurred. The weight of the financial stress was heavy on our shoulders and the whole endeavor had become too much work for me to do alone, but I could not afford to hire help. I could barely pay my team and my sales force was paid by commission only. Stuck in a catch 22, overworked and exhausted, we had to stop the bleeding and decided to let it go.

It was the first time in my life that I had been in charge of a team, or owned a business, so I blamed myself for our downfall. It was a very emotional decision to close it down and a disappointment to my team and supporters.

Stuck in reactive mode for too long, I was unable to plan out a stable future for the magazine. If I would have allowed myself time to pull back and see the bigger picture rather than spend all waking hours immersed in production mode, I would have foreseen and possibly been able to take different actions. But that was a long time before I knew anything about creative time, self-care, and making time on your schedule for envisioning and planning your goals. I'd just gone for it—as best I knew how at the moment.

I resisted bankruptcy for the longest time. It was not an easy decision to make. It was more painful to go through the legal procedure and the finality of it than it was to actually close the magazine. Although a bit sad to see this chapter of my life close, I was relieved to gain my freedom back. I had not realized just how exhausted I had been when spread thin under my many hats. I had been so involved with the day-to-day operations of keeping the magazine afloat that when it dissolved,

I was left with nothing for myself. My cup was empty and I was an emotional mess. It felt like a failure and I took it hard. I remember crying a lot and being stressed out in the months leading to our court date. I hadn't allowed myself time to rest in years. I had too many things on my plate and needed to simplify my schedule.

It was after the magazine that I tried yoga for the first time as I struggled to find my center again. What a revelation that would be.

I had performed many 'firsts' in my family – the first women to ride a motorcycle, first to move to a different country, first to sell everything and go live on a sailboat. I pushed myself outside of my comfort zone many times, but that had always been away from the prying eyes of others—always alone or with my husband by my side. Being in the public eye with the magazine made it even harder to shut down. I had to answer everyone's questions, continuously feel the heaviness of failure on my shoulders, and try to tune out the echoes of people's judgments… or were those my own thoughts?

Still, through it all I have no regrets and consider Real Sailors magazine a great accomplishment. It helped me discover many things about myself. For instance, I could create something tangible from an idea in my head, that I have the ability to carry it through, that I could develop the confidence to talk to strangers, I could put myself out there and rally people behind a cause, that people liked to read what I had to say, and that I could let go when something did not serve me anymore. All valuable lessons that I needed to learn as I moved on to the next stage of my life.

To this day, I still run into dedicated fans who tell me they safeguard copies of our magazines and miss our gatherings. Just last month, eighteen years later, a friend I met through the magazine posted a photo of our signature t-shirt on Facebook, and that made my day!

I'm glad I did it.
Moving on.

LESSON: Simplify your schedule and leave yourself time to rest and care for yourself. When you don't, you slowly become accustomed to being overworked and running a full-on schedule with no respite. Your body is always in a state of running, and your mind doesn't have time to unwind. You may not even realize when your dream job has become a ball and chain.

Like many Americans, I got caught up in my busy life. The busier I got, the more disconnected I was with my inner feelings because I was in a constant mode of reacting to the events happening around me. Boat races, events, yacht parties, regattas, contests, deadlines, deliveries, client meetings, writing, billing, editing, creating, and running a business. I did not have a single minute dedicated to my health and welfare or for creative vision work. I wasn't in tune with my heart the way that I am now, and for me, it took a tragic event to make me realize that I wasn't happy anymore and needed change.

When 9/11 tragically stopped the world, it also stopped me. I may have been thrown into a panicked financial crisis, but I also realized that I was tired and overworked, and my life revolved around a paperback.

Today, when I find myself working long hours and running from one client to the next, I consciously choose to pause and breathe. I play a mantra (a sound, word, or group of words that are repeated over and over as invocation or incantation while meditating). I choose one based on whatever personal needs I have at the time), take a yoga break, or do a meditation, I ask clients for extended deadlines, I set boundaries—all to stand firm on my commitment to myself.

Simplifying my schedule means using time management tools, or at the least creating an excel spreadsheet to manage projects. It's starting a time budget and keeping track of where my time goes so that I can analyze it and determine if I spend it being productive and focused on growth. It means booking, "me time" on my schedule as if I were a client. It means putting a daily reminder alarm on my phone to take a midday break. It means not answering the phone after hours and teaching my clients to respect my time (and teaching myself to respect myself).

I've learned that I am not the sum of the number of things on my TO DO list. Instead, I've created a TO BE list.

All of this requires that I let go of something that is simply not working for me anymore. No matter how much I cared for it, planned it, wanted it to succeed, or how much time and money I've invested in it. It means reassessing any commitments that are not aligned with my heart and learning to say, "No" to what drags me down.

I've become aware that TIME is the thing that I cannot change in life, so now I am mindful of how I spend it. When I invest time in myself, the return is much more prolific than when I spread pennies everywhere else. There will always be projects, clients, and demands on my schedule, but when I start the day by taking time for myself before others, I give myself permission to be the best that I can be. I invest in my self-worth and I am worthy to be #1 on my schedule.

QUESTION: How do I self-sabotage?

 ACTION: Schedule some Me Time

Successful entrepreneurs, athletes, and CEOs have this in common—they know the importance of relaxing and that inspired ideas rarely come after 12 hours of staring at a computer, but rather when you are relaxed and enjoying life. Creativity thrives and flows in playtime.

Your homework is to schedule a minimum of one hour per week, preferably two or more, where you will relax in any which way you prefer, as long as it is completely disconnected from the rest of the world, and you are by yourself. Mark it on your calendar and block off that time, so you do not book anything else in that time frame.

Commit to this appointment as if your life depended on it—because it does. This time is not to be missed for any reason. It is the most crucial time of the week and surpasses everything else because it is when you will create your best and highest life. You must take this time out of your busy day, to do something fun and relaxing by yourself. It can be some type of meditation or a quiet walk in the park. While you do that, allow your heart and mind to be open and listen to your inner voice for inspiration, messages, and guidance. Reflect on your current situation and write down any ideas that come to mind. This is how your inner vision will come to life.

11. Tight Quarters—
Wisdom of Crew Selection

Simplify your Relationships

With our good friends Jean-Pierre and Gina on Windsong.

"Some crew members deserve to walk the plank.
Prevent mutiny, rid scoundrels from your life."
—Carole

Once Eric and I realized that taking people in our 41 foot of living space for an extended amount of time was easier said than done, we had to make the hard decision of who to invite and who to leave at the dock.

Imagine how difficult it would be to spend two weeks inside the space of an average American household kitchen with two additional grown adults and all their own quirks, habits, opinions, and behaviors. That's on top of already dealing with your spouse, and don't forget the dog.

Add to that the fact that most of the time, we are surrounded by water, on board a moving vessel which people are unaccustomed to, and often face surprise weather systems, a mini-crisis, a close encounter with the animal kingdom, or other incoming boaters.

It's tricky to help guests understand the importance of respecting the boat's energy management system, our limited water supply, the sewage treatment systems, emergency procedures, radio procedures, and boating etiquette. Oh, and that this is our home, not a vacation rental.

Guests must listen to everything that the captain says, and do as he asks without questions. The moment "shit hits the fan," guests must be able to trust that Eric and I can pull our weight, and have their backs in the face of trouble.

We needed to make sure that we could get along great with our guests, and enjoy their company 24 hours a day, and they must respect our small personal space. Since we're also on vacation, we're not their chef or housekeeper, so we needed our crew to clean up after themselves, take turns cooking meals and doing the dishes, and actively help with regular boat maintenance.

Plus, very important to us was that our guests would need to make everyone laugh, be fun, and have a natural ability to play. Those were hard criteria for most anyone in any circle to meet.

We learned our lesson after a few weekends with people who had the wrong attitude. Either they were the biggest slobs or their negativity permeated everything like a dark cloud.

You can probably see why we decided not to charter the boat, and why we've only taken a few couples out for extended amounts of time on Windsong.

Life on board is magical, and a real privilege. With that, there are some rules and enclosed systems we have to respect. We have been blessed by great relationships with dear friends, with whom we've traveled extensively. Choosing only certain people to share Windsong with doesn't mean that we do not love our other friends dearly, just that we know we cannot please everyone, especially in such tight quarters, and it takes a unique fluidity between people to flow on board in a boating routine.

Sharing similar values in these conditions is important, and if guests have any negative behaviors that nag us before they climb aboard, there is no way they will survive a few weeks aboard a vessel as my crew.

Simply put, I respect where everyone is in their lives, I value, and honor all my friendships and relationships, and I respect myself even more—which means I will protect my inner sanctum at all costs.

Gone are the days where I try to please everyone. I know I burned myself out this way, and got stressed over unreasonable expectations. Nowadays, I look for ways to recharge myself first, then accommodate my guests after, just like all airlines instruct passengers to do—put on your own mask first.

My relationship with myself is even more crucial than my relationship with others, and that means knowing what I need and allowing myself to ask for it. Even if we are on a trip with others, if I feel the need to be alone or do something that is not in alignment with everyone's schedule, I still do it. I learned to honor my needs because it makes me a better, happier host, friend, and lover.

One of my favorite me-time activities is diving. I could spend hours, even days, if you'd let me, hooked to a hookah, swimming through reefs and fishes looking for wrecks and signs of treasures. There is nothing like the feeling of suspension you get from the water, to be immersed from the reality you know, your senses dulled by saltwater, yet your mind feels more expansive than at any other place on the planet. You are floating in a sea of water that connects you with all the continents in the world. It is truly ethereal. It transports me. I emerge from this back to reality, recharged, refreshed, and highly connected with life.

Even with a full crew and a dog, I learned to stay regimented in my practice and always found time to recharge with precious alone time, everywhere we've traveled. I'd take my yoga mat and walk to the bow of the boat for my morning meditation, or go to a deserted beach and do my morning yoga. I love to read and I spent hours devouring books as we bopped away to our destination, deliciously appreciating the rare gift of time.

I've meditated while sitting on top of the boom in lotus pose, in water up to my belly, and even while looking at abandoned shipwrecks surrounded by dolphins and sea creatures, and I've done yoga on countless beaches and shores. I wanted a crew who understood this about me—that I needed this time by myself without question.

My captain understood that, and we gave mutual respect for each other's needs and space. We allowed each other to do what we wanted and accepted that we are two separate individuals with different needs, with mutual love as the base of our relationship.

I'm not into complicated relationships. I believe that when it's right, the energy flows, so when there are complications and resistance, your attention is needed to assess whether the relationship - friendship, business, or romantic - is indeed worth it. Of course, Eric and I have had many disagreements throughout our thirty year relationship and our fair share of very low lows. We have both changed and grown at different paces which often created rifts and tension. We have a tremendous amount of compassion and acceptance for each other, and we no longer push our expectations on each other. We put our cards on the table, talk, and make decisions. And when a decision starts to conflict with one of our paths, we kindly release the other person from their commitment. This is another way to simplify a relationship. It is a great blessing we all have, the freedom to choose to be with one another. This gift has allowed Eric and I to move through some pretty tough times without the heaviness and demands typically put on a romantic relationship.

We've given each other the freedom to explore our lives separate from one another and without judgment or punishment. Telling your mate, "It's ok to leave me if this relationship doesn't serve your highest good anymore. I only want your happiness." is a sign of true love.

(I'll dive deeper into navigating the highs and lows of our romantic relationship in book #4 of this series.)

Intensified in a small space, you quickly learn a lot about relationships.

I wasn't always selective about the people (and energy) I allowed in my inner sanctum and this reflected with disagreements, disappointments, stress, and drama. I learned how truly important it is to be aware of who I bring into my personal space. A positive tribe will emanate a positive vibe and determine how smoothly you sail even through the storms. Surround yourself with scallywags, and you may find yourself abandoned in shark-infested waters at the first sign of troubles.

A boat is a microcosm of the world outside, choose your crew wisely.

 LESSON: Simplify your relationships. Let go of the need to please everyone. You'll never be able to meet everyone's expectations. What other people think of you is none of your business. Yes, you should expect love and respect from your loved ones, however, support and understanding don't always come with it. Accept that. If you are happy with your life and the decisions you've made, stop letting other people's opinions make you feel anything less than the amazing human being that you are.

If any relationship is stressed because they criticize and dislike what you do, then step aside and ask yourself if it's worth your aggravation. Even when it's a family member, you can minimize contact with them until you are able to find clarity and bring back some peace.

It is impossible to please everyone, especially when you are following your dreams.

Always remember—people's negative responses to you are merely a reflection of their own inner fears, insecurities, and lack. All things that only they can change, and until they do, you (and everyone else in their life) will be their target of projection.

You may have caused hurts in your past, and those people you've hurt may hold you as the same person you were all those years ago. That's part of their story, not yours. Let their version of the story go. The same holds true for people who have hurt you. That's your story not theirs, so it's just best to forgive and let it go. You have the power to choose who you have a relationship with. If they only bring drama, keep on sailing, sailor.

QUESTION: Who are my biggest supporters and cheerleaders?

 ACTION: Feel your Friends Game

Who do you surround yourself with? Who do you allow in your inner sanctum? Are they naysayers or supporters? Recognize how people make you feel.

Play this game: in your mind's eye, bring up each of your friends and family—one by one. Visualize each of them in front of you, and immerse yourself in the space created around both of you. Observe how it makes you feel to be in their presence. Observe the subtle physical signs, your breath, your heartbeat, how your shoulders stand, and what feelings you may experience. Notice if you feel better or brighter or even elevated in their presence. Do you feel the same, neutral with no signs of change one way or the other? Or, do you actually feel worse than before you visualized this person? Notice any signs, no matter how subtle. Do you feel weight on your shoulders, does your breath become constricted, does your chest feel closed off or even slightly restricted, or does your outlook seem less positive? Or maybe you're sitting straighter, you feel a smile come across your face, or you feel excited and upbeat? All observations have value.

It is important that you become aware of how individuals make you feel so that you can decide whether a friendship that is anything less than neutral can be reassessed and possibly limited, or even discarded. Why would you want to surround yourself with people who make you feel bad?

Not all relationships in your life are there for your highest good. While some are there to teach you lessons and instigate change, others are there to fill an inner void, typically stemming from the fear of being alone, insecurity, or low self-esteem. It is important to observe and be aware of how every relationship makes you feel and what each person brings into your life.

You know that feeling you get when you meet someone for the first time, and it feels like you've known them all your life? It's an instant connection. Make sure you pursue these relationships; there is already an energetic connection between you, a positive vibe. Explore these friendships over lunch or tea. I believe people are put on our path for a reason, and if it feels right, reach out to them. Like a flower, just add love, and watch it bloom.

12. Running with Dinghies—High Times and Funny People

Simplify your Activities

I'm nestled between Scott and Luann DaSilva, and Mark Reeder (R) at our first dinghy run event.

"For every era, the magnitude of the drama reflects your inner landscape." —Carole

The flurry of Real Sailors magazine caught on quickly. For those few years as an editor and creative director, I was in charge of bringing joy to readers and boaters while figuring out how to be a first-time business owner. We were on a constant lookout for creative ways to enjoy our hobby of being on the water. The whole magazine was produced on board Windsong and printed at a local shop in Fort Lauderdale. My team consisted of boaters, either liveaboards or long-time aficionados. Our mission was, "Saving boaters from a boring day!" and it was the only boating magazine dedicated to making you laugh.

After only one year, we had subscription holders across the US, Canada, and the Caribbean. We even had a distributor in the Turks & Caicos! This was before social media or cell phone popularity, and yet we had an active website with over 23,000 organic hits, which was quite the accomplishment. We were featured in Latitudes and Attitudes, an international cruising magazine, which gave us a boost in visibility. I was proud of our success and wanted to gather our readers to celebrate. But what could we do in the spirit of Real Sailors? I'm good at rallying people together, so events and parties became part of the curriculum.

Our first sanctioned event was a dinghy run that rallied two dozen tenders on and around the New River in Fort Lauderdale. To give you an idea of the rambunctiousness of the crowd, we got thrown out of the national park where we gathered in the morning BEFORE the dinghy run officially started.

Armed with heavy-duty water guns and some disguised as pirates, we roamed the river for hours, doing the "loop" from the New River all the way to the Dania cutoff canal, stopping on the Fort Lauderdale flats for some R & R, and pit stopping at different locations. It was actually a party on the water, with beer and strategically placed bathroom breaks. Our final destination was a local bar known as The DowntownerFlats,a that graciously hosted our crew of salty riff rafts. Folks from three different counties joined us. We had pirates complete with swords, eye patches, and fake parrots, alongside wrenches with fishnet stockings, bikinis, and bustiers. Not the typical sight on the Intercoastal waterways of South Florida! It was a parade of outlandishly costumed buccaneers with water guns on a hot summer day. Boy, did we create excitement in Fort Lauderdale that day!

One thing we hadn't planned on was having to host a rescue. To add to the excitement, an unfortunate event popped up when a participant's tiny boat got swamped by a large, rude yacht that didn't slow down and overtook the ladies in their dinghy under the bridge. The currents under bridges can be quite strong, and even though they were going at maximum speed with their small 4hp engine, that was not enough to overcome both the current and avoid the large wake the yacht threw at them. He sank their boat, sent the two ladies for a swim, and never stopped. Fortunately, the dinghy behind them was a large, powerful, inflatable boat from one of our advertisers, and the men on it jumped in and rescued the overturned ladies. Sadly, one of the women had to go to the hospital for stitches from a gash left by the prop blade. She met us later at the restaurant and assured us she was ok – what a trooper! We never found the boat who swamped her so we couldn't report him. Some people go about their lives at ramming speed without paying attention to the effects their actions have on others.

We made sure our survivors won the grand prize for showing up to the gathering after such an eventful afternoon. This momentous day represented wild times, people embracing life, unpredictable adventures, and crazy fun!

Our first event was such a success that the whole Fort Lauderdale boating scene (and beyond) started to talk about it. A lot of people said they'd be there for our next event, so we would have to outdo ourselves. In the meantime, I was invited to attend Powerboat Race Week behind the scenes, local regattas, and nautical events. The calendar of events filled up and life became a blur of parties, events, commitments and deadlines. I pushed on…

Our second dinghy run was set in Islamorada and started at 10 am at coordinates N 24* 56.95', W 80* 36.02' (that was in a shallow bay behind our friend Bobby's house). Requirements to enter included: proper boat safety gear, ID, sunscreen, hat, water gun, cooler, snacks and chart reading skills for those who wanted to know where on earth the starting point was! For a $5 entry fee, our boating enthusiasts entered a raffle for a chance to win door prizes, including an actual dinghy, a gorgeous stainless steel cooler, boating supplies, and a multitude of knick-knacks, t-shirts, and souvenirs donated by our generous sponsors. We had treasures to share and the participants would need a map and a boat to get to it!

A few weeks prior to the event, Eric along with our good friend Bob drove down to Islamorada, one of the Florida Keys about 100 miles south, and borrowed our local friend Bobby's boat to scope out locations and map out the trajectory of our run.

On the day of the event it was pouring rain in our general vicinity of Miami and Broward and the weather channel announced a flood watch. That may have deterred a few souls, but The Keys have their own weather bubble, so contrary to what everyone thought, the downpour did not cloud our day, and Islamorada saw a scorching, beautiful sunny day with pristine water and clear skies. A rowdy but friendly crowd of 70 seafaring pirates and wenches showed up on Bobby's dock that morning. It was a sight to see!

We had a multitude of activities planned for the Jolly Roger crew to explore the islands—complete with drill practices for surprise attacks, water gun fights, evasive maneuvers, and bead amassing contests.

The Keys are the most beautiful battleground for this kind of play!

All gathered aboard their rafts and got underway after one of our ceremonial wenches fired an actual antique pistol. And the run was on! Tonka, the island star and favorite white Pitbull, sported sunglasses and beads and led the race on the bow of daddy's (Bobby's) boat.

A friend of ours was flying his Ultra-Light plane over our fleet and gave tours at each pit stop. We had calculated four pit stops, similar to a poker run, except each stop included a contest people could play and try to win. In between the stops, it was a race to see who would get there first and who could drench each other the most with water guns. Goodness, a lot of laughs were had! Surely we drowned our adulthood in saltwater that day. HA! HA!

After a few miles, we came to our first pit stop. When Eric and Bob had been there to set up the course, it was the most beautiful deserted beach on a small private island far away from civilization and prying eyes. The problem was, they forgot to consider the tide, so our first 'landfall' ended up being in about three feet of water. That's where we had planned our Mullet toss contest. Mullets are a breed of small fish used to 'bait' sharks. Yes, why not tease some sharks by throwing dead bait in three feet of water while 70 people wait to see what marine life comes to bite their asses?

The goal was to have people throw the Mullets into the live bait well about 10 feet away, but 95% of people missed and their Mullets ended up in the water. Since we were supposed to be having this on a beach, the extra three feet of water made it all the more difficult and even a bit scary with the fact that we were actually bait fishing at the same time!

It was hilarious to see the participants try their hand at holding and throwing the slippery, slimy fish while maneuvering the small ocean waves. Only one person got it in, and he won first prize. It's a good thing one of our sponsors was a company that made biodegradable soap specially formulated for saltwater, so we had an impromptu lather up contest after the fish toss to see who could create the most bubbles. This scene inspired more uncontrollable laughter along with some indecent exposure moments. It's a good thing this happened before the iPhone era!

We decided to leave when a few people complained that something had bumped up against their legs in the water. We couldn't take the chance of having someone turn into lunch, so off we went to the next pit stop. Because we were now at high tide, our next stop was completely underwater (Note to self, ALWAYS check the tides tables when planning on-the-water events!). My carefully crafted schedule was soon becoming obsolete. We continued on to the famous RumRunner tiki bar on the other side of the island for more racing, more water gun fights, more flashing and bead throwing, more laughter, and of course, more screaming giggles.

I was sneak-attacked by a pirate who had filled his water cannon with ice-cold cooler water. NO FAIR! Oh, my God, that was quite a jolt to take in a 90-degree bikini!

Our hoard of buccaneers disembarked on the pier at the tiki bar to the amusement of tourists and bystanders. Some of our participants were dressed as pirates (in partially decorated bathing suits, of course), most were loud and silly, and you couldn't stop chuckling at the jokes and teasing that was rampant in our lines.

We had made arrangements to reserve the private beach by the tiki hut, and as we all tried to chill out in the shade of a few palm trees, we enjoyed fun entertainment and drew prizes for everyone. The generosity of our sponsors, and the effort my team and I had put into all of this was truly incredible. We had meticulously planned all activities and packed every minute of the day—only to realize that we couldn't control everything, especially with a large crowd. Winging it last minute was just as fun as having it all executed precisely as envisioned. It was okay that we couldn't do all the planned stops, that we were late on time, that people wanted to connect and talk rather than tackle another activity. It became clear that I had unnecessarily over-planned our day and instead could have easily sat back and not fussed over a lot of the details that caused me stress.

Now that the prizes were awarded and the pictures for the magazines were taken, the pressure of making sure everything ran smoothly was gone. Under the scorching sun, the rum was flowing and the Jell-O shots went down like cool peace into my soul.

For our one last hurrah, we all hopped in our dinghies and moved the group to the infamous Islamorada Flats, a scene for continuous parties since the 1800s! Participants needed to cool off and relax—including me, so we canceled the tug-o-war and let everyone mingle and chill in the waist-deep tropical waters. Just spending the day in this setting would have been enough to satisfy my soul, but I always felt I needed to cram as much as I could into a day to make it happy. The false belief of a young soul...

I kind of lost my bearings there for a little while after that. As everyone else talked and hung out, the sun, stress, and alcohol went to my head. I remember coming back to life while eating a hot dog in our friend's tiniest inflatable, by the smallest BBQ I had ever seen, under the cutest little umbrella. Jon of the Mountain was grilling and fed the over-served like me from the side of his boat.

It was almost dinnertime, and we were all sunburned and overserved—it was time to call it a day.

If you would have met me in those days, I could out-drink a lot of men, but that day had proved too much for me. I really needed to get myself back under control. Frankly, I needed to learn to chill the fuck out—without a cocktail in hand. I was under so much pressure from life (but mostly myself) to perform, to make this second annual event a success, to make everyone happy, that my focus was on everyone and everything else but me. The only thing I knew how to do to relax was drink alcohol. It was part of all our activities but it wasn't actually making me happy, it was just a habit created out of years of misleading ingrained social behavior.

It was also an unconscious way for me to hush my inner voice, who was not happy and tried to give me signs. I wasn't ready to listen. Not yet. So I packed my days with non-stop events and activities and when the end of the day came and I found myself at home, exhausted, unwinding with a bottle of wine. A familiar story for a lot of people in our culture where daily cocktail hour is an acceptable way to relax but only emphasizes the disconnect between us and our daily challenges.

 LESSON: Simplify your activities. I used to subscribe to the idea that the more stuff you added on top of the cake, the better it tasted. I've discovered that simple, wholesome ingredients are the key to a fulfilling experience. And so it is in life.

It's a myth that the more activities you cram into your day, the happier you become. The busier I got the less happy I became, even when most of those activities were fun. I had forgotten the importance of simply BE-ing. I found myself in the same predicament as years before when Eric and I were sitting on the beach after a night of partying and wondering why we felt like crap. If you subscribe to the concept that constant partying means a happy life, then I should have been joyful. But I came to realize that all I had done was change the scenery and move to a different crowd. Parties were a momentary activity that numbed away the exhaustion my soul felt. We were doing the same activities, actually lots more of them and now with a boating crowd. Yes, we had a lot of laughs, and I have no regrets. But I do wish I had taken the time to enjoy the simple pleasures of life instead of constantly running from one activity to the next. When I think about those days, I'm almost out of breath. No wonder my body later put on the brakes. I had no time to recuperate between one activity to the next.

Nowadays, a 'good time' for me means sitting in a tea shop with a friend and having a meaningful conversation. It means sitting around a fire with a few friends singing old tunes and playing guitar. It means hiking with Eric on a trail with the dog running in front of us. It means a Sunday drive in the mountains discovering new sites, and maybe a stop for a bite to eat. And it definitely still means a walk on the beach—that has been a constant.

Your playtime needs to reflect where you are in your life and what you feel like doing in your heart. It's ok to go all out and have the grand old time, go ahead and party like there's no tomorrow if that is what is truly in your heart to do that day.

But if you find that your days are filled with back to back activities because it helps you avoid looking at the emptiness in your heart, then maybe you need to pause your busy-ness to assess.

The never-ending list of activities on my calendar weren't there to make me happy; they were there to please my husband, or friends, or the crowd all for business purpose, promotion, editorial content. They were just part of what I did, something else on my TO DO list. Busy-ness had become an activity in itself. If there was space on the calendar, then there was room to book more events.

I had become so tuned out from myself that I could not see that I was exhausted and unhappy. But I had not yet learned to spend time doing wholesome activities to bring me joy. I was still discovering myself and unfocused on inner happiness. This was a fun part of my life until it was fun no more.

How do you unwind and fill your cup? Are you on a non-stop train, never able to pause and relax? Do you fill time to avoid and numb out? Do you have activities that genuinely fill your heart with joy?

If your spirit is deflated and you find yourself losing your footing or perhaps the parties are getting out of control, maybe those activities do not resonate with you anymore. It could be time to reassess how you spend your downtime and recharge your battery. Every year we grow, and we change, that means our activities and interests will grow and change along with it.

For every era, a magnitude of parties reflecting your inner landscape! When I was younger, I loved loud parties, loud music, and could dance for hours. I still do! I replaced heavy metal for Kundalini mantra music, biker parties for yoga festivals, the music is as loud, and I now hit the dance floor with Shakti energy (primordial cosmic force that moves through the entire universe, permeating everything with the vibration of life).

Whatever ways you want to spend your leisure time, know when it's time to move on and try something different. Stop doing that which does not resonate with you simply because that's what you've been doing your whole life. Embrace change and discover a new side of you. Playtime is where we raise our vibrations so that our trillions of cells are full of happy energy. Enjoy the heck out of it. When it stops making you feel 100% fabulous, move on.

QUESTION: What do I love to do for fun? What do I want to try?

 ACTION: The power of the Serenity Prayer

The Serenity Prayer is a powerful prayer written by the American theologian Reinhold Niebuhr. It has so many beautiful layers of meaning, but for me, it's about simplifying your life into two categories: the things you can control and change, and the things you cannot. It's also about the art of letting go. There is great surrender in it. It is very dear and holds a special place in my heart.

The best-known form is:
"God, grant me the serenity to accept the things I cannot change, the courage to change the things I can, and the wisdom to know the difference."

When you are faced with something that is troubling or challenging you, take a moment to sit, breath and repeat the Serenity Prayer. Really put your intention behind the sentences and mean it. Explore what you can face and change in your situation, and be curious about what you can accept and let go.

You can replace the word, "God" with Source, Creator, Universe, Goddess or anything that makes you feel comfortable.

13. BOAT = Break Out Another Thousand

Simplify your Finances

Always something to fix on a boat!
Eric with long-time friend Bob Brown aboard My Fair Lady.

"You can do anything you want in life, as long as you're willing to sacrifice something. What are you prepared to pay for your dream?" –Eric Fontaine

Living on a boat may seem like a cheap way to sail away from financial commitments. But think again. It is an expensive lifestyle unless you live at anchor and freestyle everything. We had no idea what we were getting into when we bought Windsong. Thank goodness Eric is an all-around expert mechanic, electrician, plumber, and sailmaker because owning a boat can cost a fortune in upkeep. Not to mention how expensive it is to dock a boat in marinas.

You may ask, well, why didn't you live at anchor? It's free! That may be true, but it's also true that we'd have to dinghy to land three times a day to walk the dog, drag laundry up the ladder of the boat, down the ladder into the dinghy, up onto shore, then walk with our bags dragging to wherever we had parked the car, then drive to the laundromat, waste half the day doing laundry. Then reverse the process and pull the clean clothes back into the small boat to get to the big boat (and hope it doesn't rain) and do this again for the groceries, errands and anytime we wanted to go anywhere. Forget about bringing ice cream back to the freezer before it melts.

And I would have had to get up at dawn to get the hubby to and from shore to go to work, and pick him up at night so I could keep the dinghy with me and not be isolated with no way to get to shore –unless we bought a second dinghy = more money, more upkeep. We'd also have to pick up friends every time they visit, and pretty much lose hours and hours of lunging stuff around, food, laundry, people and ourselves. HA!

I'd rather pay the hefty price of a marina and spend my time doing more important things.

Yes, on the weekends and vacation, it's incredible to live at anchor. But when we were back in working mode with clients to meet, rain or shine, we preferred living in marinas. We've lived in some pretty exceptional places over the years, and moved around quite a lot, a perk of living in a boat. From busy tourist waterfront, island lagoons, private mini marinas by the beach, or the quiet Keys lifestyle, we loved it all. But let's be frank, it probably cost us five times what the boat is worth, but who's counting?

When we left South Florida, we paid almost $1,000 a month for four pilings at a marina with two parking permits for our cars. Thank goodness the boat was paid for in just nine years, but before that, we also had an additional $1,107 monthly boat loan to pay on top of that! Ouch! We really wanted that boat! We paid the price of a small house in interest only, and if we would have put that money towards a house instead of 20+ years of bumming around in marinas, we would have a nice $350,000 home clear to our name with tons of equity.

The insurance can be outrageous as well, especially if you live in a hurricane zone like we did. It's a deluxe car payment every month. And there's no way around it, marinas require it and you must protect your investment.

Parts are ridiculously expensive. They are the same parts as RVs, but because they are 'marine grade', they cost four times the price. If you're not handy or independently wealthy, this lifestyle may not be a wise choice for you.

Our boat lived in the hot southern waters, which required that we have it lifted out of the water, using a giant sling at a boatyard, so we could add a bottom paint to combat the growth eating away at the hull. This was scheduled every other year, along with monthly maintenance in the form of divers cleaning the bottom and occasionally changing the zincs (zinc anodes are placed on shaft, rudder, or prop to protect the metal on the boat from electrolysis which is a form of corrosion). We could probably have done this ourselves, but couldn't find the time because we were busy making money to pay for the lifestyle (ha!).

My goodness, I have no regrets! We were well informed and made the conscious decision to invest in an extraordinary life. It was our choice. And yes, the amazing travels we did when we could take off and leave, "dock life" behind were incredible.

I am very grateful that I found a way to make a living anywhere in the world as long as I had the internet and a computer. But Eric had a high paying job and needed to be close to shore to work, so marina life was a great compromise.

We made sacrifices and simplified a lot of our expenses to pay for this lifestyle. We crunched a lot of numbers, and I made spreadsheets to keep track. I've always been organized with my finances, so we knew what we could or could not afford. It was a big stretch for us, but we made it work. Buying our boat was the dream of a lifetime—and what's money, if not something to help you realize your dreams?

LESSON: Simplify your finances. Take a good look at your finances. Always know your numbers, what you owe, and what you receive. And always give yourself some leeway for the unexpected. Knowing where your money is, what you can commit to, what you can borrow, and what your credit score is at all times, will help you feel in charge.

Never sit down to pay bills or organize your finances when you are stressed. Enter your money space with a calm mind and a peaceful heart. Make financial decisions after doing a short meditation or a few calming breathing exercises if necessary.

There are no bad numbers. There is just your judgment around numbers. Numbers have no feelings; they are simply numbers. If you don't like the numbers you see, you can work on changing them. Take charge of your finances; don't hide away from them. Organize your paperwork, buy a planner, keep a monthly budget, get your credit report once a year, keep track of what you owe, and regularly save—even if you have debt. Simplifying your finances can make the difference between happily managing your money and dreading the chore.

Taking charge of your money shows the universe that you care, respect life's currency, and are ready to live in the flow. It surrounds you with an attitude and energy of prosperity, and that is the first step toward receiving it.

Whatever your dream is, if the numbers don't quite reach your goal, and you are truly committed to your heart's purpose, have faith that the universe will collaborate to make it happen. I hope you'll take a chance on yourself. I'm betting on you!

QUESTION: If money were a person, write a letter telling them what kind of relationship you would like to have.

 ACTION: Money Mantra

Write down the following Money Mantra (or make up your own) on a card and keep the card with your checkbook. When you write out checks or pay bills online, repeat it to yourself and use it to connect with your creditors expressing sincere gratitude for offering you their services, and connect with the money in your bank for allowing you to support your dreams.

"Thank you to my creditors. I send you this money with gratitude. Thank you for this abundance. Money always flows. I save some and I spend some. I am a magnet for money. May it come back a thousandfold in expected and unexpected ways. And so it is."

14 - Hurricanes Rock— Hold Onto Your Socks

Simplify your Drama

"Be the calm in the eye of a storm." —Carole

October 2016,

I write this chapter as I sit on board Windsong and hurricane Matthew is howling outside. A category 3 monster storm with winds of 120 mph. We are fortunate that the eye is staying offshore, and we will be spared the worst of it. My work table is on a swivel, and I have to hold on to it as we rock back and forth, so it stops slamming against the mast. I stuffed a few sofa cushions between the wall and the table, and it's secured against the settee. My dog Dozer is sitting on me, anxious at experiencing his first storm, so I sing soothing songs, and we share a distracting egg sandwich. He would be nervous now whether we were in a stranger's house or on board in familiar surroundings. Animals are more sensitive than humans and still very connected to Mother Nature. I feel bad for him, and do my best to comfort him realizing we are all at the mercy of Matthew.

The good thing is that for the first time in 20 years, we're not docked on the coast, but 28 miles inland on an offshoot of the St. Johns River. We don't have many neighbors in the marina and we're next to a wildlife reserve, which means we don't expect other boats to get loose and ram us, and the only flying debris will be organic matter such as trees and branches.

We've prepared as much as we can: provisioned, filled the water tanks, loaded up on gas, tested the generator, tripled the lines everywhere, taken the dinghy out of the water, secured or removed everything that is outside (cushions, cockpit windows, coolers, seats, electronics, coolers, etc.). We've analyzed wind data and figured out the direction of the winds—which changes throughout a storm—so we could add more bumpers and more lines in the appropriate places. We've moved one car to higher ground and away from any trees, and made plans for evacuation should we need to. My ditch bag is ready to go, packed with the important stuff, and a few days' worth of clothes. Food and the dog's backpack is lying beside it. My laptop is backed up on an external hard drive, which is in storage, along with anything else we didn't want to keep on the boat.

We lost power around 2:00 this morning, but most boaters are self-sufficient: cold plate refrigerator, generator, battery banks, and our propane stove have assured us the comforts we take for granted like a hot meal, cold refrigerator, a/c, and a hot shower. We hold 250 gallons of water which is enough for two people for two weeks if we're careful. I love the sound of the wind howling outside and the rocking of the boat. Call me nuts if you'd like, but this is not our first rodeo; with 20 years of living aboard in the South Florida area, we've been through countless hurricanes. I'm not saying that it's always a good idea to stay aboard a boat in a category 3 hurricane! I'm saying to prepare for all possible outcomes and make plans accordingly. Use your intuition and common sense. We know what the boat can sustain, and we know what we, as humans, can live through.

The clubhouse at the marina is open and there are a few people in it. Our next-door neighbor offered his house should we see Matthew change track and take a direct aim.

It's now 11 am and the worse of the feather bands are starting to come in. Windsong is creaking and heeling back and forth in our slip as the wind howls and hurls at us. Bands of rain pound the fiberglass hull and resonate through the boat. It's loud and all sounds are amplified by the water we float on, we hear the rigging twisting and cracking, the lines stretch, and the stays adjust themselves. We recognize and expect these sounds from any sailboat in a storm, but it's still impressive and nerve-racking nonetheless.

Windsong is splashing in the water as happy as a clam in the mud. Sailboats are made for wind and waves. They will sustain more force and abuse than a human ever will. Countless stories are told of sailors abandoning ships for fear of their lives and being rescued at sea, only for the boat to be found months later drifting unscathed, slightly battered but whole.

The Morgan is a boat built tough, with a thick and forgiving hull. We've hit reefs and ran aground many times (not that we're proud; just a fact), so I know how solid this boat is. But it's an illusion to think we are safe and secure anywhere we are. Of course, you prepare, make plans, and use common sense, but no one can tell you when your boat will sink, which roofs will crumble, or what tree will fall in a storm. It's not because being aboard a rocking boat in a storm is uncomfortable that it is unsafe. You have to make sound decisions based on the knowledge of impending weather, and your intuition.

Our biggest concern is actually tornadoes. There's no hiding from those if you're on a boat or in a house.

As the storm wails, I'm texting with a girlfriend who lives aboard a houseboat a few miles south. It's her first hurricane on board, and we're sharing experiences, connected by our unique lifestyles, and by this hurricane coming at us. Not a lot of people will understand the enthrallment of being so close to this display of power from Mother Nature. Or of being on board a floating vessel in a storm, and being ok with it. I guess only a sailor would understand.

The sound of the howling wind, gusts and rain bands hitting Windsong brought me back to the last hurricane we lived through. I swore then that I'd never ever stay on board for another one…yet here I am…

>>> *Flashback 2005* >>>

It was Sunday, October 23, 2005 and volatile hurricane Wilma was predicted to make landfall as a tropical storm, possibly a category 1 hurricane, on the south west Florida shores that Monday afternoon. She threw forecasters a curveball by quickly intensifying overnight and became one of the most destructive storms I have ever lived through.

We were docked in Dania Beach at the time, by Martha's restaurant, which sat closed and abandoned on the Intercoastal, just north of Hollywood Beach. Seven of us, all friends, rented a five-slip marina and made it our own little private resort.

We spent the previous day running errands, gassing up the cars, filling up on groceries, and preparing for the storm. We had to secure everything on each of our boats, taking sails down, adding anchors and lines, removing every piece of movable equipment and hardware to store below. Anything that could fly off, or move and cause damage or chafe, had to be removed or secured. The picnic tables were flipped upside down and tied, chairs stacked in the shed, and plants were hidden away. The property was left naked, with strange-looking bare hulls floating in their slips.

Still, we were all cautiously positive about the storm and its projected path, based on the news forecasters, who seemed confident it would not be a major event. Even our friends and neighbors, who always evacuated at the first sign of storms, had decided to stay on board their boats. Predicted to make landfall around Naples, we were more than 110 miles away, making us feel safer on the East Coast, as hurricanes typically lose strength the moment they hit landmass.

Eric had beached our dinghy in the shallow waters, next to the property. It was tied securely between the mangroves and would hopefully stay put for the storm. Except for our neighbor's dinghy, which remained floating behind his houseboat, to be taken out of the water early the following morning, we were ready.

Or so we thought.

I woke up right before dawn to category 3 hurricane-force winds coming our way. The surprised TV anchormen now told everyone to brace for impact, as Hurricane Wilma re-intensified overnight with winds near 120mph, and gusting up to 150mph. It was already too dangerous to evacuate and travel the roads. We had to hunker down and stay put.

It was the first time in 10 years of living aboard and many hurricanes that the forecasters completely missed the ball. The path of Wilma was catastrophic; 62 fatalities and $27.4 billion dollars of damage. In Hollywood, it was the most damaging storm since 1950, with winds from 80 to 100 mph (130 to 160 km/h), lasting about five hours.

The howling winds woke me up around 5:40 am. I turned on the TV and heard that it was just about ready to land around Marco Island, with sustained winds of 125mph. I'd just about shit in my pants. My stomach knotted up, "Fuck, we're in for it now" I thought to myself. Heart racing, I woke Eric up, with our nervous dog at my heels.

The only thing we could do this late in the game was to wait it out. Storms always feel worse when it's dark outside. That hour before the sunrise you can create a monster storm in your head, and scare yourself to death imagining the worst. The TV weather people didn't help at all as they were exploiting the drama, even showing pictures of previous storm disasters to emphasize the news. I wish my yoga practice had been stronger back then, as I could have used some pranayama (yogic breathing exercise) to calm me down. I fixated on the weather forecaster's updates, the storm building up outside, and a storm of stress building on my inside. I was almost grateful when we lost power.

By 8 am, it was a mess outside. At 8:30 am, the Miami International Airport reported a wind gust of 92 mph. I was keeping track of the barometric pressure in the captain's log, and my next notation was completely off the chart in the margins of the book. It was incredible; the central pressure brought by this storm decreased 88 millibars in only 12 hours. It would later set a record at 882mb. A normal rainstorm might lower the pressure maybe 29 millibars. When you see 88mb falling in 12 hours, you take shelter and hide your valuables because what's coming is massive.

Around that time, the nearby Holiday Inn reported structural damage, with part of the roof blown off and leaks throughout the building. While the National Hurricane Center reported a wind gust of 111 mph, Wilma had just come ashore around Naples, on the other coast of Florida, and hurricane-force winds extended 90 miles from the center, with tropical force winds 230 miles from it. We were 110 miles east north east, and as it moved inland, we experienced the brunt force of Mother Nature.

South of us, the city of Key West, was under 3 feet of water, and a storm surge of 5 to 9 feet was expected on the coast. Trees were falling everywhere.

We were experiencing outer rain bands and sustained winds of 74 mph. We weren't panicked but in a state of heightened frenzy, keeping vigil on the elements through the hatch and portholes, and sailboat's navigation instruments.. The amount of rain and wind gusts hitting us in waves was incredible. It was raining horizontally. It rained coconuts, branches, and light fixtures, door panels, shingles, you name it. Not everyone in the neighborhood had done their best securing everything, and it affected everyone's safety. But even secured, the ravaging wind was too much for a lot of things. Our neighborhood's metal shed from across the street started to fly away piece by piece. It would have cut anyone in its path in half.

Downstairs, new leaks sprung everywhere. I had towels wrapped around the bottom of the mast, portholes that were habitually dry, now crying up the storm. Tupperware and rags were stuck in every corner. Dingo had nestled himself between me and the cushions and looked up fearfully every time a wind gust heeled the boat. I felt so bad for him, and us, but there was nothing we could do but hold on.

We're not sure how fast the winds were blowing over Windsong because we were hiding below. Gusts of 95mph were reported at the Fort Lauderdale-Hollywood International Airport, which was about five miles away. The stronger the wind, the more Windsong leaned sideways in its slip. Going back and forth like a savage beast trying to break its hold. The storm was showing up at low tide leaving us lower in the slip and closer to the finger pier and its pilings. Add to that the force of the wind which was pushing us against the dock, and the boat couldn't stay upright. We were bare pole sailing without canvas, tied to the dock.

A huge gust came, and we heard and felt a loud bang. Eric had to take the boards out of the door and pop his head out in the cockpit to investigate. I was really concerned and didn't want him out there; there was so much debris flying around. A few minutes later, and another large gust came, keeling Windsong so low that the hardtop we had recently installed over the cockpit, crashed against the pilling. Down below, things that had never needed securing before, even in harsh sailing conditions, were falling out of their nest. Bang! Bang! The $10,000 new hard top crushed itself on the pilling like a hammer on a nail.

I was curled up on the settee, snugged against the cushions, dog panting beside me, and another howling blast came, heeling us way low, and sending a large bottle of red wine that was secured on a shelf behind a 3 inch lip, crashing on the floor in front of me. Glass went flying everywhere, red wine spilling every which way. The dog was trying to climb on me for reassurance. We were on such a slant that items that had never moved before were now falling. Eric was in the companionway, halfway out, assessing how to stop us from completely shattering the top. I screamed at him to throw me my shoes, I was barefoot. The dog wanted to go down and run to hide in the room, but I had to hold him because there was glass everywhere. Eric came down, put the dog in the back and helped pick up the sharp pieces. I cleaned up and emptied the remainder of the shelf, holding on with one hand and securing items with the other. The storm raged outside, and we felt the roof getting crushed with every hit we took.

I didn't want Eric to go out, but he had to tighten the starboard lines and move us farther from the dock. Thankfully, he could do this from the relative safety of the cockpit, somewhat protected from the very same hardtop he was trying to save. It was impossible to do this by hand, the force of the wind was too strong, so he used the winch to do it. Inch by inch, he cranked and took advantage of every little lull between gusts to crank some more. The line was so tight you could hear it creak. Any tighter lines would have snapped. Windsong slowly moved to the right. He returned drenched. But it was done. He had saved the roof.

Adrenaline was running high on the boat. My chest was tight, my breathing shallow, and my palms sweaty and cold. Yes, I was trembling a little. Then, we heard a voice through the howling wind. It was our neighbor Bob screaming for help. We opened the doors to see him standing in his foul weather gear, waving at Eric.

He had left his Carolina Skiff in the water the night before in a last-minute (bad) decision to pull it out at dawn. It was tied to the back of his houseboat, attached to the swimming platform. The same gusts that were keeling Windsong were picking up his skiff, and sending it flying in the air, only to bounce back when it reached the end of the lines (rope) to come crashing on the swimming platform it was tied to. It was caught trying to take off and land, up and down. With each landing, it was tearing the swimming platform slowly off the boat which was attached to his boat with large fasteners. As they were simultaneously being torn off inch by inch, they were leaving behind large gaping holes in the hull. The water was coming in the holes with each wave, and Bob was in a race against time to stop the platform from completely tearing off, in order to save his houseboat from sinking.

Against my strongest opposition, they went out in the savage storm to see if they could salvage the boat. They didn't care about the dinghy but wanted at least to save the platform from tearing, and his houseboat from flooding. The threat was too great; the guys decided to step out. I was freaking out, not wanting either of them to get hit by debris. Honestly, I was afraid the wind would take them away!

There was nothing to do except loosen the lines and give the skiff more room to fly, which made it land away from the boat and saved the bigger boat from more damage. Around them, tiles and debris were airborne, and the wind was so loud you had to scream to be heard.

Next door, a working steel boat was docked with two men on board. They were protected by the 100ft long hull and were outside by the pilothouse. There were always shady characters hanging out there, and we soon found out how reckless those guys were when Bob and Eric saw the first beer can fly by their heads, while they were trying to save Bob's boat. The neighbors were throwing beer cans in the wind to see how they would fly. Drunk or merely stupid, they had absolutely no regard for the fact that people could get hurt by the cans. Of course, no one except stupid people would be out there in the middle of a Cat 3 hurricane! The neighbors could see them though. Eric almost got hit by one. I imagined the headlines, "Killed by a flying beer can in the midst of hurricane Wilma," or, "Hurricane Wilma couldn't kill him, but a beer can did!"

Intense events can feel like they last forever, but this all happened within a few minutes. The men scrambled back inside, mission accomplished.

We hunkered down for the remainder of the storm. This was before anyone had smartphones, so with the power down, we didn't know what was going on outside our immediate surroundings. Mid-morning, we felt what could be the eye of the storm. For a brief moment, everything went quiet. Dingo got a tentative wag back in its tail. The wind and rain calmed down, so we got the boards out of the doorway and came out. It was surreal. The sky had a very strange charcoal color, and the movement of the clouds was odd, fast, and threatening. It felt like the sky was very low, and the temperature had drastically dropped. It was still very windy, just not squalling.

The Intercoastal was choppy and looked like a wild river. Our five boats were bobbing hard at the chop, pulling at their lines, whipping left and right.

All our neighbors were popping up for air to check on each other and assess the damage. Two of our friends, who always evacuate, had been caught on board for this storm. They had laid down on the floor and tied themselves to their mast.

The ominous clouds were shifting directions, gathering speed, and it started to rain again. We all scurried back to the safety of our boats. And around 10 am it started over again. The winds on the backside of the eyewall were as strong, if not stronger, than those early on. It was high tide now, and the ocean water started to overtake our street, flooding the beach and running down our street like a river. Our parking lot being the lowest point in the neighborhood was filled with water, and soon our boats were islands in the storm. The ocean had completely overtaken the beach and ran down the oceanfront houses and streets.

Wilma crossed the state in about 4 1/2 hours, so by lunchtime, it was over. Left behind were a lot of shaken people, downed trees, damage, debris, and missing roofs. Times like these, you feel lucky to be alive. Everyone was ok. Neighbors came out to talk and look at their property. The cleanup could wait until tomorrow. We had survived the most intense tropical cyclone ever recorded in the Atlantic basin to that date, on board a floating vessel.

The storm reached our side of the coast with winds up to 105 mph, and gusts of 123 mph were felt all the way down to Miami. The shear of the land never made an impact to dissipate the eye, like predicted. It ravaged the tri-counties. Our area was hit hard. I remember seeing the devastation in the streets, debris, branches, glass, a car completely flipped over, another by the seashore completely buried in sand, the force of the wind cementing it like an effigy. So much debris was floating in the Intercoastal. I saw hundreds of white light bulb covers from the decorative street lights, floating down the water, like giant eggs. Cushions, chairs, coolers, doors, patio furniture, garbage cans, you name it, if it could float, it was drifting down the Intercoastal behind our boat.

Hundred-year-old trees down Dania Beach Boulevard were flattened for a mile. It was so sad to see.

We were lucky to get power back within 3 days because we were docked next to the bridge, and the Army Corps of Engineer prioritizes re-establishing power to bridges and navigable waters. The whole neighborhood across the street from us was on a different grid and had to wait two weeks before getting power back on. The company I worked for shut down for three weeks to repair the roof and water damage.

I swore I'd never ever be caught on a boat during a hurricane again…

>>> return to 2016... >>>

And here I am. As I sit aboard Windsong for hurricane Matthew after it caused catastrophic damage in Haiti, I reminisce about living through hurricane Wilma, and all that we've lived through over the years. With powerful guardian angels and calculated risks, we've always been protected, a little lucky, and safe. I am grateful. This one proved to be a short lived storm causing more problems with the oncoming flood waters that follows a storm, but since we float, that didn't really impact us. My home is an island surrounded by water, and it became a source of comfort and security once again. While everyone around us flooded for weeks, so did my heart...with gratitude.

 LESSONS:

Simplify the drama by gathering the facts. Use dependable resources to assess your situation, not hearsay from friends, neighbors or dramatic news reporters. Go to a neutral source and study whatever facts you can find related to your situation. Educate yourself. Knowledge is power.

Simplify the drama by being prepared for all outcomes. Get storm ready and get your preparations done early. Having a plan in the eventuality of disaster keeps your mind free of worries. Wherever you live, each of us will eventually face the power of Mother Nature, or at least some stormy weather system. If you are prepared for different scenarios you will feel calmer, and the process will be organized and peaceful.

Stay flexible and adapt your plan to the current situation. It may be a hurricane evacuation plan if you live in a tropical zone, or having food and an alternative heating system in your house in case of blizzard in the northern states, or knowing how to survive an earthquake if you live in "Tornado Ally" in the center of the

U.S.. Wherever you are, it's likely you face natural disasters that can be handled with more ease, when you are prepared.

Make a plan of the supplies you will need, always keep non-perishables in your house and rotate the provisions so they stay fresh. Find out where the local shelters are, where high ground is, and always keep the basic survival items like batteries, battery operated radio, fans, bug spray, propane stove, etc. in a safe bin in your home.

Make a checklist of things to do and put copies in your survival bin. Remember to be flexible, as plans often change, but making your plan while you are relaxed will save you much worry in a time of stress when hundreds are scrambling in your community to get gas and groceries. Being proactive means you will be more productive, get things done quicker and get home safe before the storm comes.

Preparations will ease the fear. Clarity will bring calmness. Calmness will bring grace. And grace will ease the inevitable tensions of everyone around you.

While we're at it, let's touch on the touchy subject of death. Death is a part of life even though most people prefer to avoid talking about it. Solid preparation will also help you simplify your drama around death. Do you have a living will? Do you have a testament? If not, why? Do you have children? Do you have pets, and do they have a place to go in the event of a disaster?

Having a testament and a living will is of the utmost importance if you truly care about the wellbeing of your loved ones. I cannot believe how many people who have spouses, and kids, but do not take the time to fill out the necessary paperwork! One thing is certain in this life: none of us is getting out alive. Do it for your children. Do it for your loved ones. Do it for the sake of your pets.

Take the time to write out what you want, and make sure you talk to someone who will know where to find it. Assign an executor to your will, guardian for your children, and an adoptive family for your pet. Let your loved ones deal with the emotional pain of the situation, without having to search for your will, fight over medical decisions, or decide if they should unplug life support or not. Be a responsible human, be a loving compassionate person to the ones left behind.. Simplify their drama.

Simplify the drama by being mindful and taking actions using your intuition. In the end, you are the master of your own ship and only you can make the decisions to guard yourself against the drama in and around you. Tapping into your intuition and spending time developing your inner sense will help you navigate the dramas in life in a more graceful way. (More about this in Book #2)

Developing a daily personal practice will create the greatest impact in your life and help you remain calm in the face of struggles and challenges. Whether you choose meditation, yoga, walking, or writing when you develop a mindfulness practice, you will be able to act in the face of chaos instead of reacting. This will be the greatest shift you will ever have because you will have clarity without the clouding of emotions. To sit still in the middle of a storm and be fully engaged and aware, can save your life. Less dramatically, to bring these qualities to life's challenges will be the difference between gracefully flowing through obstacles, or being stuck at an impasse, incapable of taking the next step to resolve your problems.

A mindfulness practice deserves the utmost discipline and is the number one thing you can do for yourself to assure success in all aspects of your life.

For me, mindfulness means creating a space between my emotions, and my thoughts about any situation. If I can stop from qualifying a situation based on my fears and worry, I can be more present and detached from the outcome, controlling my reactions. I become neutral, bypassing coping mechanisms and neutralizing any inflating stories my ego may tell. I observe the situation for what it is from a detached point of view. Taming the emotions makes me more in tune with my intuition.

I am present, prepared, and aware of the possibility that I can lose everything, including my life at any time. This awareness doesn't drum up fears, nor does it stop me from taking the necessary precautions to guard against accidents or disasters. Instead, it helps me fully embrace life, appreciate every moment, and make peace with the inevitable possibility of loss and death. This clarity gives me peace, makes me more present and alive, and helps me feel more connected with life than anything else.

We will dive deeper into mindfulness and how to create clarity in peace in my other books.

QUESTION: What calms me down, what brings me peace?

ACTION: Anxiety Relief Breathing Method

The 4 x 4 breathing method, also known as box breathing or four-square breathing, is used by Navy SEALs, first responders, yogis, and health enthusiasts around the world. Don't be fooled by its simplicity, it is very effective. It is a time-honored, stress-reducing technique that is highly beneficial for lowering heart rate and blood pressure, calming nerves, and helping to focus.

It's a simple process of an inhale through your nose making sure your stomach is expanding rather than sucking in. Then exhale either through your nose or pursed lips as you contract your stomach and squeeze all the expired air out.

Sit upright.

Slowly exhale through your mouth to the count of 4, emptying all oxygen from your lungs and belly.

Slowly inhale through your nose, counting to four slowly in your head, as you feel your belly expand with air.

Hold your breath for another slow count of four.

Slowly exhale through your mouth again to the count of 4, repeating the process for 4 minutes or until you feel calm again.

15. Crabs—They Can Eat You Too

Simplify your Story

Great Isaac Cay "Ghost Town", 1998.

"Exhale fear, inhale life." —Carole

Great Isaac Cay has been called many things: beautiful, haunted, breathtaking, scary, magnificent, and dangerous. We've seen a glimpse of almost all of these characteristics. It is basically a desolate rocky island with a lighthouse and abandoned buildings in ruins. The lighthouse was built in 1852 as a showpiece for the Great London Exposition. It was transported and reassembled in the Bahamas in 1859 and stands at 151 feet. It's now automated. Local folklore claims the island is haunted by a shipwrecked boy who was eaten alive by sharks while trying to swim to shore and now roams the island. Another ghost called The Grey Lady haunts the rock island after perishing in the waters nearby with a shipload of victims. She wanders the inhabited rock searching for her baby boy, who is said to have been the sole survivor of the wreck. You can hear her moan her sorrow on full moon nights.

In August of 1969, the two lighthouse caretakers vanished never to be seen again. Some say that the forces of the Bermuda Triangle claimed their lives, adding to the mystery.

Great Isaac is located 20 miles from the closest island, where the Grand Bahama banks meet the Florida Straits, and both join the Northwest Providence Channel. Not the best place to anchor and even trickier to get onshore, it is still an interesting sight to see.

I'll always remember the first time we anchored there. It was on a stormy night with one of the most impressive lightning storms I've ever seen. We were playing loud classical music, and the crescendo was following the blast of crackling lights spreading every which way in the sky. It was the blackest night, and every time the lightning flashed, which was every few seconds, you would see the silhouette of the 151-foot tall lighthouse, standing over us looking grandiose and kind of majestically eery. The wind was howling, and although the seas were a bit bumpy, we were somewhat protected on the leeward side of the island. The vastness around us was captivating. Our friend on board had been night fishing, and he was tormented by a humongous shark who just kept stealing his fish and wouldn't go away. It was a scene straight out of a scary movie, but I loved it.

With this memory in mind, we arrived years later with another storm in tow and two landlubber newbies on board as crew. With the storm coming from the south west, we had to anchor on the east side of the island, and use the southern rock peninsula to protect us from the clashing wind and waves. The tiny island consisted mostly of very steep rock, with no beach or soft landing area. It was in itself a piece of sharpened coral protruding out of the water with a patchy area of dirt once you reached higher ground. It could have easily been made into an impenetrable fortress with just a few modifications.

It was a challenging access but a fun exploration trip for people like us. Its creepiness was charming and worth the dangers of a stopover. You had to have safety in mind and be careful not to touch the rocks, which would cut you like a knife. Our previous dog had cut one of his paws 15 years earlier so we had to be careful to climb to land before putting Dozer on the ground.

I knew from the moment we rounded the cape and anchored Windsong, that the dinghy landing would be rough because the seas were building from the oncoming storm. Eric had no choice; he had to go walk our newest family member, Dozer, a puppy we had recently rescued. But I could choose to stay and relax on Windsong. Hey! After all these years, I had nothing to prove, and he had two crew members with him to help.

On board were our friends, the Gariepys who were on vacation from Canada to celebrate Helene's 50th birthday. They didn't have any sea experience and were in the Bahamas for the first time. We had just crossed over from Florida, and there was no way they were going to miss this excursion.

There were two places on the island where primitive steps had been carved directly into the rocks to climb and access the island. On that day, the steps on one side were buried underneath crashing six-foot waves, and on the other side, they were located in a small cove-like area, where a primitive boat ramp had been carved on the island. The waves bouncing off the three-sided walls created a washing machine effect, and the rocks were so sharp that they could have busted the air chambers of our inflatable dinghy.

The captain made the decision to land on the rocky low lying peninsula.

So there they went, the three musketeers safeguarding our new puppy on his first Bahamian landfall. Mommy (me) waving goodbye from Windsong and keeping a watchful eye on them with binoculars, and the radio channel turned to 16 in case of emergency.

Eric landed the dinghy on the southeast shore. There was no beach to put the boat on, so he disembarked the crew and the dog on the rocks, tied the tender, and pushed it out to sea. The rocks were sharp so they had to be careful to slowly climb their way to land.

The first thing that Helene noticed was the hundreds of tiny crabs scrambling from the intrusion and doing their pinchy dance, as they scurried away. Disturbed by the human presence, they waved their claws up and down as if saying: "Go away, intruder!" She could not believe how many there were as if the rocks were alive with the little critters. It was an uncommon sight for her.

The old caretaker's house and abandoned buildings stood higher up in the center of the island by the lighthouse. To get there, they had to walk through a field of overgrown knee-high brush.

Eric went the long way, reaching land and setting Dozer free. Denis took a shortcut aiming for the abandoned village, and Helene wearing sandals and a sundress, followed by walking on a path created by the remnants of the old foundation and a water collecting aqueduct, which created a path between the overgrown bushes on each side.

She was entranced by this extraordinary visit, and unaccustomed to the life of a sailor, with dinghy rides, landfalls, crabs and abandoned ruins on deserted islands. Denis was excited to explore the sight.

Then all of a sudden, she started feeling little pricks on her legs, she kept waking but the more she walked the more it scratched her. She felt her dress being pulled on, and her legs being cut. In a flash of panic, she thought, "oh my god, the crabs are coming after me!" Her mind went nuts. She could already see them crawling up her legs and eating her alive! Wearing a dress she felt even more vulnerable. She started jumping up and down screaming, "AHHH! Denis! It's scratching! They're in my dress (translated from French)."

Her husband ran back to her, panicked and confused, wondering what was happening.

She had worked herself into a frenzy, and stood in the field, jumping, kicking her legs and shaking her dress, screaming to get them out, thinking there must be critters stuck in it.

When the men reached her and Helene looked down at her legs, she was surprised to see nothing. Not one drop of blood, no crabs, no scratch, no bugs. She didn't understand what happened, where did they all go? Where were the bites, the blood? The guys - always the comedians - teased her and told her she needed to take her dress off for further investigation.

When she pulled her dress down it felt heavy and bunched up and snagged in certain places. Upon closer look, Eric found that it was covered with HITCHHIKERS! He laughed so hard!

Hitchhikers are the spiky seeds of a plant that will attach to anything rubbing against it and travel along using this method to disperse and reproduce. Like sharp Velcro, they are awfully tenacious and some rather painful as well. Dozer had them all over his paws and fur too.

The crabs, fresh in Helene's mind, had set her on high alert, and her fears had taken over any logical thinking. That's when the story of blood-sucking crabs trying to get in her pants and eat her alive was born. All was well, she survived of course, but her pride took some beating with our constant teasing for the rest of the trip.

Our musketeers continued their exploration, emotions high, and tension somewhat eased. It's always an adventure with the Fontaines!

Dozer was finally free to run and release some of his puppy energy, which the boat could hardly contain. He had done really well in the crossing and was adapting beautifully on the boat. But this new playground was pleasing his curiosity, and he investigated every inch of the island, marking it as his own.

Only the sound of the birds and the wind coursing through the ruins could be heard. (And the echoes of Helene's screams!) They imagined how difficult life on the rock must have been back in the day before modern communications, and the isolation one feels in such a disconnected life, far from everything, with only the occasional boat bringing news and supplies.

The lighthouse, now automated, was impressive to see. You could go inside, but the steps to climb up had been removed for safety. The ruins told a story; where the water cistern was, a walled pen on the outskirts probably held small animals for milk, some buildings still had walls and window frames upright, and showed the magnificent clear view one had upon rising. It was truly stunning to see the surrounding ocean from this high point and made amazing pictures of boats at anchor.

The atmosphere on Great Isaac is different than anywhere else. You cannot help being in awe and loving it, all the while feeling the hair on your arms stand up, expecting to catch a sudden apparition out of the corner of your eye.

It was enthralling but the sun had set and it was getting dark. Back on Windsong, I felt they were pushing it a bit; usually everyone is back on board by dark, but the crossing had taken longer than expected, and Dozer needed his exercise. I could see them make their way back to the dinghy using another path, seems like Helene had decided not to take the short way home. Dozer was ahead of the trail happy as a clam and covered with hitchhikers.

Turning their attention to the dinghy, they carefully made their way onto the sharp rocks to leave.

While they had been exploring, the seas had built up. Now the waves, which were only spraying some water on the rocks earlier, were now crashing violently on the western side of the shore, splashing all the way over the rocks, and over them, twelve feet in the air, and spraying into the east side of the peninsula where the dinghy was tied.

Hard to get on this island, and even harder to get off.

Every other wave hitting the cliff was showering them with saltwater. The sharp rocks were now slippery and dangerous. Eric carried our puppy, and the crew carefully followed his steps, eager to get off this strange island. Helene was still getting over her emotions. When the waves came, they braced, held on and closed their eyes, waiting for the wash cycle to be over. Eric was almost to the dinghy when a big wave engulfed them, and both he and Dozer disappeared behind a wall of white water. Denis and Helene frantically searched for them, and as the water receded, they saw Eric had fallen down on the rocks, and the dog was gone. Then Dozer appeared between the rocks, dripping wet and wondering what the heck was this new game daddy was playing. Eric reached to grab him but slipped on the wet rocks and busted his knee on the coral. Skinned to the bone and blood pouring out, Denis grabbed one of his arms to help Eric up as he grabbed our soggy dog, placing him in the safety of the dinghy. Our landlubber friends climbed on board, and told the captain, "Let's get the F&%4 off this island!"

I was watching from afar through the lens and knew this had been an adventure. I was enjoying a very different scene on Windsong. Great sunset behind the peninsula, the darkness of a stormy night creeping towards us, the sound of the ocean splashing away on the rocks, the impressive silhouette of the lighthouse towering in the dusk and shining its light onto the blue sea…but I knew.

The crew that returned was a very different crew that had departed just over an hour ago. Disheveled, wet, full of adrenaline, and bleeding. Their first request was for rum, then the medical kit. Eric's knee was cut deep into the white meaty part, and crying red. He would have needed a few stitches, but we were miles away from civilization, and he's a tough guy. He's great with first aid, and with our help, we patched him up, and life was good again.

The spooky island didn't get the best of the Windsong crew, but it did claim blood.

LESSON: Simplify the story in your head. As humans, we love to tell ourselves stories and often get carried away by embellishing, turning facts into harrowing journeys, or tragic events into distorted crime scenes. If we start believing the stories playing inside our heads, we can lose track of the facts, and create a world of illusion. When we add our filters – beliefs, childhood experiences, untruths we carry within – we distort the truth into unrealistic stories that trigger our fears and make us react when there is no evidence to the contrary.

Do you know what fear stands for? False Evidence Appearing Real. Always ask yourself what the facts are, and detach yourself from the emotions. Answer with the utmost honesty. Here's an example using Helene's situation. One, I feel scratching. Two, I am on an island. Three, I just saw crabs. Four, I am wearing a dress. Solution: lift your dress and look for what is causing you angst.

Fear may feel larger than reality, but you can keep it in check by being present and aware. If you stay in your head playing stories, you will become part of the movie and react just like an actor would.

If you are not in immediate physical danger, then your fear is an illusion created by your mind. Keep your stories in check and breathe through it.

Sometimes fear is justified, and you must act to get yourself out of danger. In most situations though, the fear is greater than the event. It's the power of the imagination!

QUESTION: My greatest fears are…
Dive deeper and answer this: They may be based on…

 ACTION: Acknowledging and Releasing Fear

Try this exercise. Close your eyes and be present to whatever fear is currently affecting your life. In your mind's eye, imagine this fear taking a shape or form, some distance away in front of you. Make your fear concrete in the form of an inanimate object of color. Know that at any time you can open your eyes and stop this exercise and that nothing can harm you in any way from visualizing.

When you see the fear embodied in front of you, walk towards the shape of your fear. Stand in front of it. Straighten your back, put your hands on your hips, and stare straight at it. Lift your chin. Say out loud:

"I acknowledge that I feel a fear of _____ (insert fear) _____ .
I see you and feel you.
Regardless of you, I will still _____ (insert action)_____ .
I have power over you. You are only an emotion.
I rise above you and release you."

Now visualize the shape getting smaller and smaller, and slowly dissipate in front of your eyes as you repeat to yourself, "I release this fear. I acknowledge you. I have power over you. I rise above you. I have released my fear. I am at peace."

See it completely dissolve until there is nothing left but empty space. Walk forward, past the now empty space, leaving this area behind you, repeating the mantra, "I am peace," as you walk away.

16. Involuntary Rudder Adjustment—Sunny Islands Turn Dark

Simplify your Values

"In order to sail the ocean of life, one must recognize the oncoming tide." —Carole

After about ten years of living aboard, we changed our home port from Fort Lauderdale to the magical Florida Keys. The tropical island chain runs 120 miles south of Florida, and the last island, Key West, is the southernmost point of the Continental United States. The islands are all small, at most a few miles wide, and you're almost always bordered by the ocean from the road. On one side, it's the Atlantic Ocean, and on the other, the Gulf of Mexico. Life in the Conch Republic is truly of another world. Time slows down, stress dissipates, and the main goal of everyone is to enjoy life. Sounds like the perfect life? It can be for some. For me, it's where I felt the most disconnected from the world and became very sick.

The first marina we landed in was in a lagoon right off the ocean in Tavernier. The water was so pristine that you could see schools of fish swim around the boat. Every day I'd feed them my leftovers at lunchtime and say hi to the neighborhood lobster living on the sea wall. No one dared eat the resident crustacean and hunting for lobsters in marinas is strictly forbidden!

We had a fantastic array of fish, stunning purple parrot fish with colorful wings and orange ones with cobalt blue beaks, black and yellow striped sergeant majors, all kinds of snappers, grunts, pinfish, yellowtail, jacks, and groupers. It was like living in a giant rainbow-filled aquarium.

Dolphins occasionally played in the lagoon. It was a sublime place to live, especially after being docked in the city for so long. We went from the dark, polluted waters of the city to the crystal clear ocean. We were immersed in aquatic island nature, complete with a resident iguana who loved to sunbathe on the inhabited boats. It would take over as owner, sitting and staring arrogantly as it defied all who tried to shoo it away. It pooped all over the boats (staining the fiberglass) as it sipped margaritas with one middle finger in the air. Okay, so I made that part up, but you get the picture!

The island chain has a protective barrier reef a few miles east of it which breaks any kind of waves in bad weather, so you can enjoy the ocean almost every day of the year. It's a nautical paradise and for boaters it's an absolute dream to live there.

Eric managed a boatyard in Marathon Key, and after closing down the magazine I found a job as a graphic designer working for a manufacturer of herbal supplements in South Florida. When we sailed to the Keys, the owner wanted to keep me on and have me work remotely. Thanks to technology and the internet I worked from the boat, bobbing in our slip, hearing the constant splash-splash of the water, as the sun poured in from the hatches.

We docked in the coziest marina and we became instant friends with an amazing riff-raff of boaters who hailed from every corner of the nation. Every day, we'd gather in the late afternoons under the large communal tiki hut. It was decorated with fishnets, crabs, funny signs, fishing gear, coconuts, fake parrots, and postcards from around the world. Pastel colored island décor filled every nook and cranny of the property, and flower beds bloomed all year long. We'd smoke fish with coconut husks, barbecue, troubleshoot boat problems, and share stories, meals, and tall tales.

We splurged on a brand new Boston Whaler as a dinghy and used it to go everywhere. With only one road in and out of the Keys and from one island to the other, it was faster and easier to avoid the touristy road and travel everywhere by small boat. We sailed, swam, explored wrecks, hunted for treasures, and immersed ourselves in the laid back island life. Every night, we blew the conch horn at sunset, often hearing it reciprocated from across the lagoon. This is a Hawaiian tradition that salutes the end of the day to say thanks. We even had a neighbor who, on occasion, wore his kilt and played the bagpipes on the bow of his sailboat. Boaters are a rare breed of unique life-loving people!

We felt so much more connected with nature. Everywhere we looked the ocean smiled back. Surrounded by the rhythm of the sea, one instinctively fell into a natural ebb and flow and life slowed down.

The move to the Keys had been harder on me than expected. On the outside, my life seemed idyllic but on the inside, I was fighting a silent battle with illness and depression.

As my body struggled to regain balance after a car accident the previous year in the city, I had discovered Iyengar Yoga to help me heal a back injury. A devoted fan from the start, I took multiple classes each week, learning the importance of body alignment, core strength, and body awareness. Before we moved, a friend brought me to my first Kundalini Yoga class and it was love at first sight, or should I say, 'sit'? Unfortunately, there wasn't anything like it in the Keys. I left my first yoga community behind when we moved and thoroughly missed this newfound interest. It was still in the early days of the internet so online classes weren't yet popular or prevalent.

Despite being surrounded by beauty and water, my soul was unquenchably thirsting for sustenance. With a budding awareness and new perspectives clashing in my head, I was on the brink of a major transformation but still avoided any deep introspect. I couldn't understand why I sometimes felt so sad in the middle of this paradise.

Maybe it had to do with being faced with a closed off society that was judgmental and suspicious of newcomers? Although these folks were kind to strangers, native islanders never really let you inside their circle of friends. I missed the inclusive community I left back in South Florida, and found that there wasn't much to do in the Keys except fish or drink, two things I had lost interest in. All the good friends we made came from somewhere else. It's like there were two communities living side by side, with one giving the other the cold shoulder for not having the good fortune of being born on their island. Private clubs, private parties, closed off floors in bars that only native islanders could go to were abundant. I felt sad—not for not being included, but for the mistrust and disconnection that they were perpetuating by their actions. The world is disconnected enough without adding more boundaries between people. It reminded me of high school and it felt like a sad way to live.

Being a traveler and having lived in many places, I authentically value the friendship of everyone I meet no matter where they come from, what language they speak, or what color their skin is. I know their life experiences will exponentially add to mine. I value human connection above anything else in life, and never felt more disconnected than I did when I lived in the Keys. I longed for something to fill the void in my heart. But I had no clue how to fill it.

I thought I was ready for something new with this move, but soon realized that once again I had only traded in the scenery. I was stuck—again—in the same pattern. My husband was drinking too much, everyone around me was drinking too much. I was tired and felt disconnected with this lifestyle, with the community, with the people, with life. I was physically ill a lot of the time which made me reassess how I wanted to spend the remainder of my time when I did have enough energy to face the world.

My work also turned into a mess with my bosses' personal drama affecting business and spewing into my space. I would drive to the mainland once a week to the office and meet clients and take care of any on-site business. It had become a toxic environment with the two owners (in the middle of a divorce) often screaming at each other, or anyone on the receiving end of their anger. Even though I worked from the boat four days out of the week, I sometimes found myself caught between a rock and a hard place with the two of them working against each other. It left me uninspired and longing for something more.

I had no pastime that fulfilled my heart. Life was a only a routine— even if perpetuated in the most idyllic conditions. I was losing interest in most of the things I used to love. I had questions but no answers and felt frustrated by my health, my relationships, and the lack of support I found available.

What did I value in life? What did I believe in? How did I want to surround myself? Were these core values mine or acquired? I didn't believe in what I was doing anymore. I needed my purpose, passion, and relationships to align. I felt out of sync with a lot of things. Despite living on an island, there was a lot of noise, superficiality, and even pettiness.

Nothing used to bother me before. I used to be a big wino, and drank to unwind almost every day. Now, my health had forced me to stop that. It made me the outsider in a culture of drinkers and party goers. I was the only sober person at the party. No one wants to hang out with the designated driver—unless it's time to go home. I felt alone and out of place. Suddenly, I was the boring one. The only one who went to bed early because I could not stand to listen to any more drunken stories. Some friends even called me a party pooper. Not only was I getting sicker and sicker, I was also stressed and depressed and my favorite method of relaxing was forcibly removed.

Without the liquid bravery, I was a quiet introvert. I thought about everything. A lot of fears consumed my waking hours now as I wondered and wandered in my ever-inquisitive mind. Why was I so sick? What was the underlying sickness underneath it all? Was this how my life would be from now on? What did I accomplish while I was healthy? Would I get another chance to do all I wanted to do? Why was I so unhappy with myself and my relationship? Where had the passion gone?

It might have looked like the perfect life on the outside living on a sailboat in this tropical setting but I was tormented with pain and insecurities. I had come full circle with the girl in the pool years before and the simple question that was annoyingly posed to her then…who was I?

I was searching for myself, trying to align who I thought was, with who I had become, and determine if I liked that person.

I had lost my north star and my compass needle was spinning out of whack. My mind was telling me one thing but my heart was feeling something else. I tried to keep doing my usual activities but the enthusiasm was gone, replaced by frustration and disappointment that happiness eluded me while I was surrounded by paradise.

Surely there was more to life than working and drinking. But now that I couldn't quiet the voice with alcohol, I felt overwhelmed and unprepared to look at my life for answers. The painful truth was that the things I valued before simply did not matter to me anymore.

I was not yet equipped to handle the debilitating flare ups and sudden sobriety, so, I went numb. I'm not surprised I went into a deep depression. I wasn't ready to answer any of the questions floating in my head, especially in the middle of a health crisis. It was too much. I started taking the antidepressant the doctor gave me and everything went quiet. I didn't have any energy left within me to fight my way back to the surface. It took my all just to roll out of bed. There would be a time to face things later. For now, I hit the disconnect switch and the lights went out. I let the dark clouds swallow me.

LESSON: Simplify your values. Feeling overwhelmed, frustrated, depressed, and even angry are signs that something is out of sorts in your life. Where I was in life at the time was in conflict with who I wanted to be. Once I stopped drinking, I was faced with the cold hard truth that I was not doing well. My body, heart, and soul had been screaming for attention but the vino muted that inner voice. It was much easier to numb out than to deal with the fact that I was unhappy, face the reasons why, and take action to make changes. I didn't know that at the time. All I knew was that I felt stuck, angry, and frustrated. This, of course, was reflected in all my relationships. My life looked amazing on the outside, but some days I felt like I was living a big fat lie.

I needed to reassess my values. What was important to me? What and who did I surround myself with? What did I prioritize in my life and was it aligned with what mattered to me the most?

Some of our activities conflicted with my new priorities and interests. I was changing and growing but life hadn't caught up with me yet.

QUESTION: What do you value most?

ACTION: Identify your values

Sit in a quiet place where you won't be disturbed. Put on light music or do a short meditation before you start. Get your journal and brainstorm all the values that are important to you. Below is a list to get you started, but feel free to add whichever comes to mind. Take your time and be thorough. When you are done, try to shorten the list down to 5 of your most essential values. To further prioritize, you can score them from 1 to 5. You want to narrow down your list to help you figure out which values are most pressing so that you can prioritize them in your life and get right to the most important work first.

We are often guided by our mind and our actions or goals do not align with our values. This leaves us feeling depleted and dispirited. By getting to know what your most prized values are, you can concentrate on the ones that are fully aligned with your goals and purpose. It is the only way to stay inspired and passionate about what you do.

If your most important value is justice but you work in an environment that strips individuals of basic rights then you will never be enthusiastic about going to work. If you value security and community, you may not find happiness in isolation on a boat far away from land. Let the top three values of your list guide your actions and decisions. It can help you get unstuck when you are indecisive, and move towards a more balanced life.

Achievement	Learning
Activism	Love
Adventure	Loyalty
Community	Motivation
Consistency	Open-mindedness
Courage	Peace
Creativity	Perfection
Commitment	Perseverance
Compassion	Reliability
Dependability	Respect
Determination	Passion
Education	Patriotism
Efficiency	Positivity
Environmentalism	Security
Friendship	Service to others
Fitness	Simplicity
Health	Sincerity
Honesty	Spontaneity
Humor	Success
Independence	Time
Innovation	Understanding
Integrity	Wealth
Intelligence	Justice
Kindness	Add your own!

17. Take your Medicine—
It's Good For You!

Simplify your Priorities

"Choosing to sail above the clouds is not a dreamer's quest, it is a survival skill." —Carole

I'm starting this chapter with an index of my doctors. You'll understand why as you read along (hint: they get increasingly difficult to keep track of).

Car Accident (doctor #1)
Gynecologist (doctor #2)
Dermatologist (doctor #3)
Dentist (doctor #4)
Primary Care Physician (doctor #5)
Chiropractor (doctor #6)
Internist (doctor #7)
Liver specialist (doctor #8)
Obstetrician Surgeon (doctor #9)
Oncologist (doctor #10)
Gastroenterologist / Hemorrhoid Surgeon (doctor #11)
Who knows what—Head Doctor #12
Functional Medicine Doctor (doctor #13)

I was forced to stop drinking, it wasn't a choice. My body started to have allergic reactions to anything with alcohol. It started with beer, which gave me the side effect of putting me to sleep. Literally, I drank one beer and you'd find me snoozing below within half an hour, unable to keep my eyes opened. I would drink cocktails and wine instead. Certain wines started to make my throat itch and one day my usual cocktail provoked a small asthma attack. I couldn't breathe, my tongue and throat felt tingly and although I didn't need to use my Epipen, it gave me quite a scare. I had a few experiences with anaphylactic shock from allergies to stinging insects and certain fruits in the past, so I recognized the foreboding signs. The last thing I needed was for my throat to close off and have to use my Epipen just to have a drink. I had become physically incapable of consuming alcoholic beverages.

What I didn't mention was that this happened as my body was assailed by months of miscellaneous symptoms from an invisible inflammatory attacker. From the time I had my first car accident almost two years before, my health had been in steady decline.

At first, my symptoms seemed unrelated. The year before we sailed to the Keys, I got rear-ended in a car accident. The doctor (#1) gave me a short bout of anti-inflammatory and pain pills for my back injury, and I started having difficulty digesting. Soon after, my moon cycle became very painful, so I had to see my gynecologist (#2) about that. She didn't find anything at first and recommended I take Advil three times a day as necessary. Next, was a visit to the dermatologist (#3) because my face was breaking out. I was almost middle-aged! He said it was rosacea and handed me another prescription. My dentist (#4) treated me for gingivitis, a first for me, of course a prescription rinse and expensive treatment followed. I started to suffer from painful indigestion.

I didn't understand why I was suddenly plagued with all these different problems when most of my life I had been relatively healthy. And the fact that it was all happening at the same time raised some fears.

After these initial symptoms, I went back to my primary physician (#5), who treated me for Irritable Bowel Syndrome and referred me to a chiropractor for back pain (#6). He also ordered scans and MRIs to make sure nothing had been missed from the car accident.

Over the next four years the snowball grew. What had been problem-free periods for most of my life became excruciating to the point that my gynecologist prescribed 600 mg of Motrin three times a day. I was concerned by the amount of prescription pills I was taking and even went back twice to see her, but she reassured me that there was no side effect, and many women took this to help with their menses.

While I was dealing with all of this, my internist (#7), who did ultrasounds and MRIs to rule out any car accident injury, called me in alarm and referred me to a liver specialist (#8) after seeing disturbing results. I was in a lot of pain: my back from the accident, my stomach was constantly swollen and painful, and my lower left abdomen flared up once in a while with sharp knife-like pain after I ate. My health had become a mess!

Since the pain from my moon cycle was now all month long, my OB/GYN sent me to see an obstetrician surgeon (#9) because I could not possibly stay on pain medication 30 days out of the month.

Meanwhile, doctor #8, the liver specialist discovered large lesions on my liver and sent me in to see an oncologist (Doct #10) for an urgent assessment. DAMN, that knocked the breath out of me. Oncologists work with *cancer patients*, everyone knows that. I remember the terrifying phone call from their offices scheduling me in within three days – which had me even more scared. I barely slept or breathed until I got the results. They rushed me in for more needles, and more tests dissecting every inch of my liver. More blood samples were analyzed for tumor markers, and God knows what. My stomach was so distended it became hard to breathe. The chronic inflammation was swelling everything, including my breasts which had jumped two bra sizes and couldn't even feel appreciated! My lungs could not fully expand and I could never catch my breath.

As the months passed and I got sicker, fear was ever-present and snuffed out any feelings of happiness. I tried to keep up with life but I had zero energy for it. My time and energy was consumed by doctor visits, work (as best as I could), and rest. My soul was suffocating.

Imagine yourself locked in a very deep but small dark room with only a tiny light coming from above. As the air is snuffed out of it, so is the light. You scream and scream and no one can hear you. The oxygen slowly disappears, and you run out of air until you can scream no more. You are left weak and immobile on the cold floor. Staring at the vanishing light, gasping while everything hurts to stay alive, all the while unable to understand why you've been put in this cell.

That's how I felt. Confused. Overwhelmed. Scared.

While I awaited the results on my liver, the OB surgeon (Doct #9) scheduled a hysterectomy after he found that my uterus was three times the normal size and abnormal tissue growth had invaded my uterine walls. The adenomyosis, fibroids, and beginning of endometriosis were causing the heavy bleeding and pain I was experiencing. It was a big decision, and he was the second doctor I consulted on this. I needed relief. He came highly recommended and I hoped that he knew what he was doing. So after months of trying to alleviate the pain with pills, they cut out my uterus. Thankfully the knife-like pain (no pun intended) subsided after surgery. Regretfully, the inflammation and its after-effects remained.

I never bounced back. Still swollen two months after surgery with digestive problems getting worse, I was referred to a gastroenterologist (Doct #11) who ordered a colonoscopy, an endoscopy, and full blood work.

I walked around like a zombie with the life drained out of me and no relief in sight. I needed an overhaul. Couldn't someone just help me please? I couldn't understand why, with all their poking and prodding, they couldn't figure out what was wrong with me.

The results were inconclusive with nothing of major concern. We started playing the prescription merry-go-round. One after the other the gastroenterologist made me try all the pills he had at his disposal. I felt like a test subject ruled by doctors devoid of compassion: testing one drug, reporting for duty, changing drug brands, recording side effects, trying more drugs. Repeat. Meanwhile, my stomach was distended like I was eight months pregnant, the skin so tight it felt like it was going to burst any minute. When I tapped on it, it sounded like those red balls we played with at recess in elementary school. My whole body was wrapped in inflammation. I could not eat without having serious irritable bowels. I dreaded eating and had not been able to feed myself properly or without pain in months. You would think I'd lose weight, but I was heavier than I'd ever been. I now had red dots popping on my torso everywhere, and brown darkish plaques polka dotting my body, this of course meant more trips to the dermatologist for more creams and lotions.

My life had become a race to find answers. Unable to assimilate energy from food, even a short trip to the grocery store was an endeavor. Some days I had no energy and my only solace was the couch. I hid in the womb of the boat, rocked away, cocooning my pain away from everyone's prying eyes. I felt lost and unsupported.

I was so swollen that the inflammation was trying to find it's own way out which translated into a massive problem with hemorrhoids and a visit to see a surgeon (Doct #11) to get those removed. This proved to be a very challenging journey on its own, with multiple procedures ending with the most painful surgery you wouldn't even wish on your worst enemy. It took me six months to recover from it. Weeks and weeks of excruciating pain. I think I'd birth quintuplets before going through this surgery again. Oh, I cringe just remembering my cries every time I needed to relieve myself.

During the hemorrhoid saga, doctor #6 scheduled me for MRIs every six months to monitor the lesions on my liver. They didn't know why my liver was compromised, but it wasn't cancer. A minor sigh of relief—without the energy to celebrate. He sent me to see a diagnostic specialist, and honestly, I don't even remember what title he wore. He will forever be known as doctor #12, the kind that looks into unsolved cases, a specialist of specialists. Guess what he told me after only five minutes in his office and a quick read through my file? He said, "You're depressed."

"REALLY?! That's your freaking answer?" was my outward response while thoughts of DUH! *Of course, I'm fucking depressed you asshole – you go through what I'm going through with no relief in sight and deal with all the pain, doctors, and pill-popping and see how quickly it zaps the life force out of you!* shot through my head.

He prescribed antidepressants and told me my symptoms could all be in my head.

There I sat, buried behind a wall of sadness, I could hear myself scream, but it's like I was stuck with gooey mud filling my lungs. I didn't even have enough energy left to scream out my anger. I had become totally and absolutely numb. I could hear the waves of anger crashing inside of me but buried my head in the sand. A tear or two escaped me. I grabbed his prescription, closed the door behind me and walked away.

This was my experience with modern medicine. This is what mainstream 'health' looks like in America. While I was fading away, my life hung in limbo, resigned to be in pain. I don't know if you can imagine what constantly being in pain does to a human body. I hope you don't know what it's like to have your body be unresponsive to anything you try, to have it resist treatments, for it to refuse the food you try to give it,, and to feel like you're wasting away with life slipping through your fingers like the sands of time. I sincerely hope you don't know the deepest disgust that penetrates your every cell when doctors and 'experts' you rely on for help tell you that you're making this up in your head because their tests can't find anything.

Unable to cope, I retreated in full preservation mode, detached from all emotions. I turned off the world.

I started taking the antidepressant and allowed the numbness to wash over me. Being awake was too painful. I just wanted to close my eyes, go to sleep, and make it all go dark. I guess that's why we call it the dark night of the soul.

I cried constantly and considered that this was how it was ending for me. I had an especially good life until now, thank goodness I had lived so much when I could. But even the memories of my previous good times could not make me smile. With no solutions in sight, I closed myself off to the world.

There was some truth to what that doctor said, just not the type of truth he intended. I absolutely believe in the power of the mind. And I believe I was at a crossroads in my life which required a wakeup call to make drastic changes. However, there was a physical reason behind my symptoms. This would finally be confirmed months later with a DNA test from a functional medicine doctor—a practice built on the foundation of conventional medicine but using a personalized and integrative approach to healthcare which involves understanding the prevention, management and root causes of complex chronic disease.

The antidepressant helped but not for the reason it was prescribed. The digestive tract creates 90% of the serotonin our brain needs to be healthy, happy, and balanced. While I thought I was depressed because of my symptoms, it was the opposite. My depression was actually one of the many symptoms of my out of balance digestive system that wasn't producing enough dopamine for my brain.

New studies show that the brain-gut relationship is closely tied, even calling our stomach our 'second brain.' More research needs to be done, but it's now common practice to prescribe an antidepressant to alleviate digestive problems. So I started to feel a bit better.

Years later, I am now able to see the greater lessons I was learning from this episode in my life. The Universe was trying to tell me something, but I had not yet learned how to listen to my body or my heart to understand what I needed.

 LESSON: Simplify your priorities. If there is one thing I knew it's that I did not want to live like that anymore. Contemplating being gone and lost to all had not been what I had pictured for myself. I had always put everyone's needs before mine until I had forgotten what it was that I needed. No matter how bad I felt or sick I was, I always put work first. I prioritized my husband's wants over mine. I was living a great life, but was I living my dreams or his? The boating community was fun and kind, but was all the partying really what my heart longed for?

My body was forcing me to stop and reassess my priorities. It made it impossible for me to do anything but concentrate on myself for once. I needed to become my #1 priority and that was non-negotiable.

What did Carole need in order to get out of this dark hole? What did Carole want?

Yes, I did get lost in the dark for a while. Yet, it was in the darkest of dark that I found my courage to live.

However dim, a light steered me on a path of self-discovery. I wasn't ready to give up just yet. I needed to stop looking at others to help or save me. I needed to explore myself from the inside out—to find my wings and the passion to rebuild and truly fly.

QUESTION: Describe your perfect day in detail.

 ACTION: 3 x 3 = Choose better

Think about three choices you make each day that can be changed or modified to better your life. For the next three days, every time you're about to take that action, choose to do better.

For example, if every day you choose to sleep in and be late for work, gossip about your neighbor, and eat chips before going to bed, then choose better.

Don't make it hard, start with small changes and work yourself up. Once you've accomplished your three-day goal, notice how good you feel about yourself and journal about it. Reflect on what is stopping you from making this a habit. Step it up a notch and do it for 30 days. You can do it!

18. Double Whiplash— What Are the Chances?

Simplify your Voice

"Sing little bird, your voice will carry you above the clouds echoing through the stars." —Carole

I still see the people knocking on my window trying to get inside my car to help. My doors were locked, and I wasn't coherent enough to reach the unlock button. I saw their lips moving but I could only hear a large buzzing sound in my head and ringing in my ears. Everything was a blur and surreal, after a powerful impact snapped me at the very core of my being. I was disoriented and remember feeling like I wasn't completely in this world anymore. My fingers were tingling, or was I numb? Just a second ago, I had been listening to music at a red light on a busy intersection, excited about the holistic Ayurveda workshop I had just attended and eager to get my body on the road to recovery.

A pickup truck had just rear-ended me—again—a second car accident almost identical to the first one five years earlier. What a freak cosmic smack from a 2 x 4.

I don't know how long I was locked in the car feeling dazed and confused. It was the distant voices of people at the crash scene surrounding my car that stirred me. The fog dissipated. I was in my car and strangers were telling me that everything was going to be alright, help was on the way, and please unlock the doors!

I was hit with so much force that my Xterra slammed into the car in front of me which gave me double whiplash. I remember feeling like it shook me so hard that my spirit snapped out of my body, and like a ghost in a movie, I could not quite get back into it.

I was finally able to awaken from my stupor and unlock my door but that movement felt strange. Something was wrong. I could see the liable pickup truck with a mother and a child in my rearview window and two heads with white hair in the damaged car in front of me. The ambulance arrived as I was still attached to my car seat. It's a bit vague what happened next but I remember my head being immobilized as they got me out of the car strapped to a trauma board and rushed me to the hospital.

I have no recollection of the ambulance ride. It took me a long time to feel like myself again.

Hours later, after scans confirmed that no bones were broken, my husband was given the OK to take me home. We were both grateful that I was still alive. A MRI would later determine that I suffered a C5/6 herniated disk in my neck. I was discharged with a prescription for painkillers, which I needed and took for a few days, as well as anti-inflammatories which I refused to take. I was starting to realize that the treatments and prescription drugs were causing more harm than good and I wanted to protect my frail stomach as best as I could.

As if I needed more drama in my life, this accident would bring me down an additional long recovery route with new doctors, new tests, new therapies, and legal procedures to top it all.

I had to wear a neck brace for months and do serious physical therapy. It affected my right hand which made computer work with a mouse barely bearable to downright impossible.

This happened after my hysterectomy but before my hemorrhoidectomy so physically I wasn't in great shape to begin with. It was the curveball from hell.

The fact that both of these accidents had undeniable similarities was not lost to me—I was fully aware that something meaningful was happening to me.

In both instances, I got rear-ended while I was completely stopped at a red light, in broad daylight, at large, multiple lane intersections, with at least a dozen cars fully stopped in my lane and waiting for the green. Both times, the driver was a woman on her phone, and get this, both accidents happened on a street named Atlantic! I am dead serious. The synchronicities look like red flags, and I would go back often to extrapolate what other synchronicities in my life were simultaneously happening in other areas of my life. I was just starting to dig into the body-mind-spirit connection at this time, and studying holistic living to try to understand what was happening to me.

I thought I was on the mend and that I would regain control of my life again, but this just sent me spiraling down even further.

In the course of five years, I had gone from a vibrant young woman who loved to sail, laugh, have fun, and live top deck in the sun, to a couch ridden suffering soul who hid below deck in her cocoon of fiberglass. I didn't trust life, didn't trust my body, and couldn't trust doctors, myself or anything else in life. It didn't matter if I surrounded myself with palm trees, sailboats, or sand; life had become pain and suffering.

All these medical emergencies and physical pains happened over the course of five years. Half of those years were while Windsong, our home base, was in the Florida Keys, which meant a 3-hour drive every time I needed to see a specialist, get tests done, or undergo procedures or treatments.

Surgeries were the hardest and took months to recuperate for my frail immune system. Each of them brought on new complications and symptoms.

How did my life get so difficult? I was on a painful roller coaster and felt completely out of control. Of all the things you think you can count on in your life, your body is one you never question, especially when you're young. I got very weak and ultimately lost confidence in my body. That brought up so many questions, "What happens if I die?" "Is there an afterlife?" "If I am not my body, then who am I?" "What is the lesson behind all this suffering?" Those were my good days; the rest of the time, I felt like a zombie—numb, and aimlessly wandering through the clouds.

For my husband, the hardest thing was to watch me fade away. We lived in paradise, and most of the days I could not enjoy it. All the medications were making me emotionally numb but only partially suppressed my symptoms. He didn't recognize the happy girl he married and there was nothing he could do except try to make me as comfortable as he could.

He wanted the doctors to stop giving me pills, especially the ones which altered my moods. He hoped we could find alternative ways to cope. My body was sick, and my mind fell into depression. He finally called my parents in Canada and told my mom, "You need to come down and be with your daughter." She flew in to the rescue for moral support. I had another surgery coming up, and neither my body nor my mind were in shape to undergo the assault.

From the moment I started seeing the oncologist waiting several days to get test results hoping it wouldn't be a death sentence, to today, I had been terrified and unable to understand or have compassion for this malfunctioning body of mine.

To avoid fear, stress, and pain, I checked out. I was emotionally exhausted, numb, and burned out. I had let things get out of hand, let others make important decisions for me without listening to what my body was trying to tell me. I had been trying to avoid my feelings for so long, telling myself I'll be ok, I'll be ok. But deep inside, knowing I was far from it.

The gastroenterologist (Doct #11) I was referred to following the complications from my hysterectomy, had given me new scripts to try. When I asked him how long I was going to take this medication, he asked, "Well, they're making you feel better, aren't they?" "A little bit," I replied, to which he jovially belched out, "You can take them for the rest of your life!" I was floored. I was only 41.

I was knocked back to reality.

To what point would I listen to my doctors who obviously didn't know how to heal me? How many chances had I given them? There was no way I was going to feel this way or take medication for the rest of my life. It took me way too long to fully realize that their way wasn't working.

Yes, the pills were easing some of the sufferings, but it didn't stop the source of the inflammation. I felt disconnected from Western medicine, unheard, and uncared for. What it lacked was connecting the dots back to the source. Western medicine has specialists for every system. In my experience, they did not communicate with each other, and I had to tell them about my other symptoms which were often discarded as unrelated. The doctors were happy just to treat the symptoms with pills or, when they ran out of options like doctor #12, they blamed it on me saying "It must be in your head."

It finally became clear that they'd given up on me—just like I'd given up on myself.

I had gotten lost in the world of Western medicine and had become a case number. The system was so compartmentalized that without proper communication between specialists, my health had quickly spiraled down. Treatments were dislocated and targeted only one organ or one system, while symptoms spread throughout my body. It was not logical to disregard other ailments when the human body is a fully interdependent operating system (just like a boat, and mine was sinking!). Healing had to happen as a whole. I needed complete homeostasis, and it was becoming clear that I needed to find alternative treatments on my own.

Questioning everything, I looked within and listened.

Will I get a second chance? What will I do if I have my health back? To what length will I trust a stranger over my own self to heal my body?

At this point, my life may have depended on it. Losing my health was the biggest wakeup call. I realized that I had not taken responsibility for my health. I was raised to think that doctors know best. I had completely released the reigns to my doctors, trusting in full faith—without questioning. But they didn't. At least not with me. I was accountable for all that happened as a willing participant, for agreeing to take all those pills and treatments. That had to stop. I had to take charge. I had a voice. I had a choice.

I fired my doctors.

Damn, that felt good. It was one of the best days of my life.

Eric contacted an old friend who recommended a Chinese medicine doctor and acupuncturist, who slowly weaned me off the anti-depressant, and had me replace the stomach medications for herbs and homeopathics. As I regained some health, my mind got clearer and my body stronger. But after a while, I plateaued with his treatments and after a tense conversation where I found him to be rude and unwilling to listen to my concerns, I fired him too.

I was done hiding in the clouds and nodding quietly at yet another doctor's push for sole reasoning. I found the confidence to refuse attitude from anyone, especially health care professionals. I had been avoiding painful feelings and uncomfortable conversations most of my life because I didn't know how to deal with them.

I focused on the positive in everything while compartmentalizing everything bad, just like the doctors did. I broke down my life in little pieces and looked only at the parts I liked. What was painful, hard or uncomfortable was locked away in a dark box. I was completely disconnected from my body, heart, and soul. I was even disconnected from my treatments because I gave away my voice, and let others decide how they would treat MY body. I was finally realizing that if I truly wanted to heal, I would have to look into the dark boxes I had ignored for so long. Intuitively, I knew I needed to connect back with the pain and dive into myself before I could move through this experience. It would take courage, consistency, patience, and bravery. My newfound passion for yoga and holistic healing was giving me some tools to integrate into my life to help me face my fears and finally find the cure I desperately needed. It gave me strength and a willingness to dive deeper.

It was time to quiet down all the voices around me and rediscover what my true voice sounded like. The voice behind the fear and painful stories. The voice I was born with that was thrilled to finally have me pay attention. The voice that raised her heart to the sky.

 LESSON: Simplify your voice. There comes a time in everyone's life when you've had enough. The first time I said, "NO" out loud, it broke the dam and all the emotions I'd been holding back came crashing down into my life with determination, relief and even anger. When you're at the bottom of the pit and lost in heavy depression, anger can be a powerful driving force.

My whole adult life I tried to make everyone happy, please my husband, please my boss, and please my friends. I was a "good girl" and didn't want to rock the boat too much! (pun intended).

I may not have known what I wanted yet, but I knew what I didn't want. I did not want to feel sick anymore. I did not want doctors to pay more attention to my chart than to me. I did not want to feel like what I had to say didn't matter. I did not want to be a test subject for pharmaceuticals. I did not want important decisions about my health or my life made without my consideration.

I had swallowed my voice and my fears for so long that it had festered and infected my very being.

I did not want anyone to make me feel powerless. Ever. Again.

It was time to take a stand and let the world know how I felt. The mere thought of this was terrifying for me but it was also one of the most liberating moments in my life. The day that I started saying NO to others and YES to what I felt was true in my heart was exhilarating.

People may have a hard time understanding this hidden truth about me but I'll lay it out here:

- I had the courage to sail a 20-ton boat through terrible storms, but in my marriage I couldn't seem to find a way to tell my husband that I was worried about our relationship, that I felt disconnected from him and that something would have to change in order to have a future together.
- With my friends, the fear of losing their friendship kept me from standing up to tell them when they were out of line and hurt my feelings.
- In my career, I allowed my boss to overstep boundaries and push his personal beliefs on me.

• As for those many doctors, I wasn't brave enough to tell them I thought their treatment was a bunch of baloney.

Sometimes in the deepest darkest place, you find something that is invaluable and inspires you to fly. That's why it was important for me to open my eyes and step away from the comfortable numbness of depression and face the pain I was in. It was raw, messy and necessary. I had to become my greatest fan and biggest advocate and could only do so by speaking up and stepping up. No matter how scared I was, facing my deep dark truths meant taking responsibility for my life, and however chaotic, it was the only way to start healing and find peace.

Courage, bravery and self-love were treasures I discovered underneath an ocean of pain.

Finding my voice gave me the strength to dig them out.

QUESTION: Write down one thing you have been afraid of saying out loud to yourself or someone else.

 ACTION: BODY TALK

Your body responds differently to each emotion. Learning to read your body's language will help you become attuned with your inner guidance, helping you prioritize what's important. It will also bring space between you and your emotions and allow you to experience them instead of being directed or overwhelmed by them. Noticing physical sensations related to emotions is the first step towards connecting body and mind.

For the next week, when you experience emotions, connect with the sensations you feel in your body, observe and write down everything you feel in a journal, from any area of the body, you experience sensations. Start to decipher your body talk!

When I am angry my body feels

_____

When I am stressed my body feels

_____

When I am sad my body feels

_____

When I am calm my body feels

_____

When I am happy my body feels

_____

When I am ecstatic my body feels

_____

Relaxing body scan meditation.

The body scan meditation is a simple and effective way to ground yourself in the present moment. It can help you become aware of the subtle signs your body sends so you can learn to translate your body's language. You may sit or lie down. Simply close your eyes and imagine the breath traveling to different parts of your body. By inhaling and exhaling while visualizing and feeling each area relax. You will feel a deep sense of release and peace. The better you are at recognizing how your body feels when you are at peace, the faster you will recognize stress signals sent to you when frustration or anger bubbles up.

It is primordial to your health that you listen to your intuition and any messages that come while doing this practice. Become your own health advocate and open a dialogue with your spirit, being present to how you are feeling each and every day. Your body and intuition are there to guide you to a healthier and happier life, all you have to do is listen!

Uncross your arms and legs and cover yourself if you feel you may get cold once you are in a deeply relaxed state. Close your eyes and take three slow inhales through the nose, exhaling deeply through the mouth. Relax and feel the ground supporting you. Continue breathing normally and observe the natural ebb and flow of your breath…in and out…and as your heart rate comes down, your breath slows down. Let go of any attachments to thoughts which may arise, and release any judgments…relax your mind… allow yourself to simply be, get connected with your breath, in and out.

Bring your attention to the path of the breath starting at the tip of your nose, entering your nostrils, coming down your throat and entering your lungs. Follow the exhale as it leaves your chest cavity and out the nose, moving the tiny hairs inside your nostrils.

Observe this path for a few breath cycles.

Now bring your awareness to your left toes and relax the toes. Notice your left foot and relax the foot. Feel the left ankle, and relax it. Notice the left leg and consciously relax the entire leg.

Move about your body this same way and relax every part. Scan each side, starting at your toes and travel upwards, spending the time of a breath on each body part. Breathe into your buttocks, hips, lower back, abdomen, ribcage and relax. Your torso, relax. Scan each side traveling down your arms, elbows, wrists, hands and fingertips and relax.

Feel your scalp, relax your hair. Notice the ears, relax. Feel your forehead, and relax. Unclench the jaw. Relax your eyebrows. Feel your lips and relax the tongue in its mouth. Notice the eyelids and relax the eyes in its socket. Relax your entire head and neck.

You are completely relaxed and at peace. Take a moment to enjoy the sense of release you created and listen for any messages your body would like to express.

As you familiarize yourself with the body scan meditation, create a deeper experience by traveling inside the body and visualize your inner organs and systems relaxing. Visualize your stomach relaxing, intestine, liver, tight muscles, nervous system, blood vessels, heart relaxing, etc.

The longer and deeper you go, the greater the peace you can achieve and the more aware and in tune with your body you will become.

19. Filling the Tank— Your Body, Your Vessel

Simplify your Gut

"If you slack on the maintenance, the ship will fail."
—*Carole*

A working boat reminds me of our bodies. It has all these intricate enclosed systems that need to work in conjunction with each other for optimal sail. If one system fails, it affects another, then another. You may be able to function for a while, even cut off the jeopardized system, but eventually you're going to need to rely on it and if it's not fixed by then you won't be sailing anywhere anytime soon. You need to be mindful of what you're doing at all times, because what you do affects the whole boat.

Windsong has an enclosed water system. We have two 100 gallon tanks and a 40-gallon hot water heater. We need to fill the water tanks with potable water about once a week at dock, or we can stretch it up to two weeks, when we use it in moderation when cruising or at anchor.

One day, after almost ten years of living aboard Windsong, I was outside with the water hose using the tool to unscrew the deck water cap to fill the tanks. I remember struggling more than usual to get the lid opened and thinking, "Why does Eric tighten these so much?" When I finally got it opened, I stuck the water hose in and turned it on full max. I needed to keep an eye on the water gage in the master cabin closet below to know when it's full, and switch the hose to the second tank, so I went downstairs and watched the gage.

I stared at it and didn't understand why it wasn't rising. I tapped on it a few times, took a flashlight and pointed at it and waited for the water level to rise. "It must have been REALLY empty," I told myself. I had been filling the tank for at least 5 minutes at full capacity, and the little floating ball was still at zero. Hmmm…I went back on deck to see if the hose had possibly fallen off, but no, it was still in the thru-hull. Then it happened—at that moment I realized that I had put the water hose in the wrong tank.

I was pouring water into the diesel tank.

Oh MY GOD!!!!! NOOOOOooooooooooo! Damn right, I did. What a colossal mistake! I poured gallons and gallons of water in our diesel tank at the complete dismay of my husband. What a dumb move. I own it. It wasn't one of my proudest moments. I can laugh at it now, but I felt terrible about it back then. The disconnect between me and my actions resulted in almost tragic consequences for our motor. The same disconnect happened with my body, resulting in painful consequences. If you fill your tank with the wrong fuel (or water), your boat will be spewing and choking before it dies. Not only will it stop working, it will really damage the systems, possibly break parts, or even mess them up beyond repair.

Fortunately in this case my husband's quick thinking saved the day. He disconnected the hose at the bottom of the tank (the one that connects the tank with the motor, and since diesel is lighter than water, the water had gravitated to the bottom of the tank. So he drained it until the diesel started to come out, and saved the rest of the 60-gallon fuel.

The same truths applied to my body. Before getting sick, I had never paid attention to the foods I ate. I didn't eat badly, but drank and ate whatever I liked. I didn't care about nutritional value, or what those drinks and foods could be doing inside me. I had a somewhat mainstream American diet, except lighter on the fast foods. Then I took all those prescription drugs for an extended amount of time, and never thought about the side effects on my system. I trusted my doctors when they said there was no harm. I just expected my body to work on low quality fuel, while shoving time bombs down the tank. I was completely disengaged with how my foods made me feel. Actually, I was disengaged from how I truly felt about my life.

After firing my Western medicine doctors, and starting my holistic journey, I experimented with different healing modalities like biofeedback, herbs, infusions, supplements, vitamins, muscle testing, acupuncture, steam baths, Ayurveda, Kinesiology, Reiki, sound healing, N.A.E.T., even weekly enemas! Yikes! It was a long journey but still easier than the one I'd been through. I was beginning to hear and trust my intuition which told me the key to true healing had much to do with connecting and integrating my body, mind, spirit, along with healing foods and nutrition.

I was eating consciously but without knowing that even some healthy foods were causing me harm. I still had a lot of symptoms and was on a merry-go-round trying to find answers, but I had hope and felt empowered by having taken charge of my healing.

I had become very fearful of eating though, to the point that I didn't want to eat anymore. It wasn't quite a phobia but I had a huge reluctance about eating. Food was my enemy. Every time I ate, I got sick. I felt good before a meal, so why would I want to eat knowing that for the next few hours, I'd be zapped of energy, swollen, or crampy, or gassy, or all of the above? I'd get up in the morning feeling good, then I'd have breakfast, and it all went downhill from there. But I instinctively knew that food would also be my savior.

I saw an ad in the paper announcing a celiac and gluten-free support group and a gut feeling told me that I had to check it out. I had no idea that the functional medicine practitioner who ran it would become a life savior, or that the DNA test result she would have me take would shed light on most of my problems: I had a Celiac gene and a gluten sensitive gene. That meant each of my parents had one of these genes, and that most likely, there were other people in my family silently struggling with symptoms of indigestion and inflammation, which was later confirmed after a quick survey.

She explained that although not Celiac from birth, I was at the beginning stage of a full blown auto-immune disease. If I continued with my current diet, it would further damage my digestive system and long-term health and cause some irreversible damage. (I was already there with the loss of my uterus.)

I was grateful beyond words because I finally had some answers and could now turn to solutions. Oftentimes the blood tests the doctors administer give false negative results while DNA testing is the most accurate way to know if your body reacts to gluten. A huge relief washed over me.

Do you know how it feels to finally get a glimpse of a healthy life after YEARS of struggling? It meant that I could live pain-free, leave the darkness behind, come back into the light. It meant that I could BREATHE a full breath, completely inhaling and exhaling without obstructions. I could get my freedom back. I could enjoy myself and maybe even realize a few dreams that had been discarded in the trash. Getting hope back was profound. Without hope there is no vitality—only darkness and pain—no will to live. I could allow myself to feel again.

While we were awaiting the test results, this doctor had me start a food diary. It was time-consuming, but the single greatest tool because I learned what foods my body was reacting to, and what made me feel better. It had been previously hard to diagnose because it wasn't just one category of foods which caused me pain; it was a whole range of products. And the combination of some caused extensive inflammation, which lasted for days.

Writing the food diary made me mindful of what I was eating. I became a detective. I asked my body questions in the form of food and got replies in the forms of reactions. Slowly, a pattern emerged, and I learned to decipher my body's language. I observed what made me feel good and ate more of these foods, avoiding the reactive ones. The tricky part was figuring out the culprits because there was more than one. I remember cutting out labels and fact panels and sticking them in my diary looking for a common ingredient.

Something new came up almost every day. I was diagnosed with Candida overgrowth. Candida is a fungus that aids with digestion when colonized in proper amounts. When overproduced, it will create most of the symptoms I was feeling. The only way to heal from this is to go on one of the strictest diets there is. My goodness, the list of things I had to give up actually brought me to tears on quite a few occasions.

Not only did I have to remove all gluten from my diet, I found that I was also lactose intolerant, could not digest any red meats or fatty meals, and reacted with allergies and sensitivities to sweets, sugars, alcohol, fruits, caffeine, nightshades, tomatoes, potatoes, yeast, mushrooms, pasta, creams, bread, and prepackaged food. It was nuts! (No nuts included—Pun intended!)

It was a huge life change and I struggled with it. I had the choice of eating what I wanted and staying sick, following a path that would eventually graduate to full-blown autoimmune disease, or I could change my eating habits and get on the road to recovery. But breaking 40 year-old habits is easier said than done, especially when you're the only one eating like a monk and have to deny your taste buds on a daily basis and reprogram your brain to want the bland foods you are allowed.

My functional medicine doctor put me on a regimen of supplements, mass probiotics, and herbal remedies to reverse and heal the damage done by the pharmaceutical drugs. They had destroyed my stomach flora and created a toxic environment where my food sensitivities bloomed.

The gluten exposure led to leaky gut syndrome, where the ingested gluten attacked the tiny cells in my stomach lining, and the resulting inflammation allowed toxins to leak into my body through my intestinal walls, affecting the integrity of all my systems, and slowly poisoning me.

Because everything starts in the stomach, and it was compromised, I was at the mercy of the foods I ate. The dairy caused gas and more inflammation, adding mucus throughout my body and made me feel like I had a constant cold, sneezing for hours after a meal with a runny nose, and it gave me acne. Pork, beef, and any fatty meats caused the most excruciating pain in my lower left stomach; felt like I was being knifed. My doctors had called it colitis. The depression could even be traced to my stomach flora, as the primary source of serotonin producer, my gut had not been producing enough, so my hormones were completely out of whack. The Candida had been the most difficult to figure out because I was reacting to a wide range of foods. It thrived in the unbalanced environment perfect for its nature.

We formulated a plan, and I had to rethink my diet based on a shortlist of foods allowed on a candida, gluten-free, dairy-free, red meat-free, alcohol-free, caffeine-free, sugar-free diet.

I went through a wide range of emotions that first year, from excitement at finally getting a diagnosis, to sadness and frustration at giving up the foods I loved, to anger and out loud rage at knowing that surgeries and years of pain could have all been prevented. If I had known sooner that I had a problem with gluten, I could have prevented the inflammation, the leaky gut, the compromised immune system, and I would have avoided the hysterectomy, the liver lesions, the most painful hemorrhoidectomy, the months of post-surgery recovery, the years of chronic inflammation, the days and days of crying and feeling miserable, the time lost being sick instead of living and loving my life.

And the fear. The damn fear of dying, of eating, of living, of doing anything that would trigger pain. It got so that I didn't trust my body, I didn't trust food, I didn't trust myself anymore because I hadn't recognized the signs, and lost my zest for life. The mass chronic inflammation was my body's response to its attackers: gluten, dairy, and anything that bloomed the Candida. But my mind's response had been fear, withdrawal, disconnection, distrust, loss of confidence, and finally, deep depression.

I had a lot of healing on my plate.

What woke me from my numbness, besides getting off all the damn pills, was anger. I was mad at the doctors, at the health care system, and at myself. Anger can be a great motivator and drove me to find solutions doctors had been unable to find with their limited ways of looking at health.

My body was weak, but I listened and changed my whole pantry. I was determined to learn everything about nutrition and superfoods to boost my healing. You spend your life eating and rarely stop to think that it's sustaining you, giving you life. You get hungry, you eat! But what if it could do more than satisfy a need for a full belly? What if it could nourish, help you thrive, feel energized, and heal what was possibly ailing you? Could it be that simple?

The first few years were the hardest. I was healing not just my body, but my heart and soul. I felt like I'd been through a hurricane, an earthquake, and a tornado all at the same time and left starved and shipwrecked on a deserted island. At least I didn't feel like I was drowning anymore, but I was emotionally exhausted. And honestly, the restrictive diet was difficult to get used to.

A friend showed me a beautiful meditation to do before eating to help bring back mindfulness in my relationship with foods. I needed to reconnect with my food and my body. With just a short pause before eating, I would connect and thank where my food came from, thanking the earth, the farmer, the people who made it readily available to me. I blessed my food. That also helped me to stay away from processed foods. I'd much rather thank a farmer than a laboratory. I honored the source of my healing, and what was sustaining my life.

I started to feel better, and was now entirely off medication, only using supplements and nutrition to support my system. My tank now filled with clean fuel, my body was beginning to regain strength, and my brain fog lifted.

Things I dismissed and things my multiple doctors did not correlate, now made sense. I have my functional medicine doctor to thank for that, for making me realize that if we search for one common source, one common thread; we can resolve all problems. My skin problems were related—despite the creams my dermatologist prescribed. My hysterectomy would have been avoided, had my gynecologist asked about the reason I had Adenomyosis. My liver lesions would have stopped growing if my oncologist had questioned why my liver was so stressed. I would not have needed an extremely painful hemorrhoidectomy surgery, if my gastroenterologists wondered why I was subject to such inflammation. The specialist would not have dismissed my depression and prescribed an antidepressant if he would have researched that stomach distress was also depleting my serotonin (a neurotransmitter necessary for mood balance, which contributes to wellbeing and happiness, primarily found in the gastrointestinal tract). A lack of serotonin has been proven to lead to depression. Everything is related and interconnected. All. The. Time.

It had been a very long time since I had felt like myself. I had days when I was so happy to be alive that I would cry out of gratefulness. There was a new lightness in my heart and I felt like I had been given a second chance. I was taking charge of my life and seeing positive results. This was the dawn of a new day—the dawn of a new me!

We humans have a tendency to complain about a lot in life, but the moment we lose our health, we realize that nothing else matters. Without our health—we die. Not even a floating paradise could save me from that. You sink your battleship. Game over.

I felt like a bird getting its wings back after years of being caged. With tears of relief washing down my face, I could gaze into the clouds and slowly learn how to sail above them.

 LESSON: Simplify your gut. Signs from our bodies are here to help us align ourselves with our highest life, and we cannot accomplish this without our health. Simplifying my gut meant my diet was the number one key to regaining my health. To function as a whole person, all aspects of my system must work properly, and I am responsible for doing everything in my power to provide a healthy environment for my body to thrive and be healthy. Bringing mindfulness into my eating habits, I take ownership of everything that goes into my mouth, things that affect my environment, my own level of awareness, and my overall well-being.

Simplifying my diet meant getting back to basics, shopping the store's perimeter, eating only healthy perishables and easy to digest wholesome foods (as nature intended), and making simple meals.

Simplifying your gut also means listening to the signs your body is telling you. Pay attention, write them down, observe, and see what your gut feeling is telling you. Your body is speaking, are you listening? I'll dive deeper into this in book two.

QUESTION: What is my body telling me?

 ACTION: Start a Food Diary

If you have any health issues, commit to keeping a food diary for a minimum of 30 days. Before you say, "I don't have time for this!" ask yourself if you have time for a six month medical leave or years shaved off from living a fulfilling life. Carry this journal with you everywhere you go, and write down every single thing that you swallow. You see, everything you ingest affects your digestive system, thus your health. So include your meals, drinks, gum, coffee, vitamins, snacks, medications, etc. Think of it as a month spent picking up clues and learning your body language. Notice feelings of discomfort, stomach ailments, or distress, but also note what makes you feel better, more energized, or clear-minded. Immediately remove from your diet the foods which cause you pain, discomfort, or make you feel sluggish, foggy, or tired.

Go further and investigate everything which comes in contact with your skin: creams, lotions, soaps, shampoos, deodorant, etc. Replace all personal beauty products with natural alternatives, and explore benefits you feel when using essential oils.

If your health is really challenged, commit to a 3 to 6-month diary to decipher the patterns and cycles and understand your body better, add notes on emotions, cycles, life challenges, and stressful situations.

You must become your own detective and health advocate. Becoming aware of the subtle shifts in your body and/or energies when you ingest certain foods or use particular products will change the way you look at nourishments and beauty products and change your relationship with your body. Recognizing how you genuinely feel in your physique is the first step to transforming your life because you are practicing mindfulness. Do not take other's consensus on a product. What worked for someone else may not be suitable for you, and what people say didn't work for them could be an important key to your improved health. You must get to know your body, and feed it with the intention of healing it.

Heal your relationship with your body by coming from a place of compassion, love, and forgiveness.

Conclusion

"When simplifying our life, our mind can rest so that our heart can find the song of our soul. Its music will guide the way."—Carole

Late in August, we took our Boston Whaler for a late Monday morning ride. It was an outstanding day. We passed the Coast Guard station on our way west from Snake Creek, observing seamen eagerly washing and keeping up on boat maintenance. We waved at fishermen going out the inlet, their ice chest filled with hope. We admired the coastal homes up and down the channel facing Windley Key with their hammocks and palm trees gently swaying in the wind and some folks gardening or watering their yard. The morning light on the water reflected like diamonds on everything. Such a laid back place to live, such peace and beauty. Today, this felt like paradise.

We veered off into the mangroves and skidded on a plane through the shallow waters of the Y shaped inlet barely avoiding the overgrown branches from the skinny channel. There wasn't much traffic on the water. The speed and warmth of the sun on our face felt invigorating! It was a magic carpet ride!

We didn't know where we were headed. I held on to a bow line and gazed out onto the sea. We were on the Gulf of Mexico, bayside or west of the island chain. Out of a beautiful white cloud just north of us, a rainbow appeared. We made a decision: today we would be chasing a rainbow! Half an hour later, we came upon a shallow area in the middle of the bay, a mile away from shore and prying eyes. There was a small patch of sand surrounded by seagrass, like a small pool clearing in the middle of nowhere. We stripped naked and jumped in with delight. The rainbow was still shining bright, and the sun was hot on our backs. All sorts of fish swam around us, curious about our surprise appearance. In that moment, I remember telling myself how amazingly blessed I was, embracing Eric, and telling him how much I loved him. Not all days were as bright and beautiful but I'll remember that one forever because it was the first day I felt good enough to go out in weeks.

When we climbed back on board, we saw three bottlenose dolphins playing in the sun and swimming large circles around us. Dolphins, rainbows, my lover, and the ocean—surrounded by luck and love. The entry in my journal that day says: "I'm so in love!"

I had not felt this hopeful in months, maybe years.

Who was I at this present day you may ask? Someone who was simplifying her life and in the process of letting go of all the rubbish that blocked her view of who she truly was. Someone deeply listening to her body, heart, and soul, and trying to navigate towards a better and healthier future. I was not perfect, and had failed myself in many ways, but as I finally recognized my reflection in the water, I smiled, forgave myself, and promised to be kinder and gentler to who I wanted to be.

This was a new beginning. Gifted with a new perspective on life, I treasured my newfound hope and determination to live.

The sea called on me to expand my horizons and there was no way I was going to decline this enticing offer.

"Anchors up and raise the sails! Adventures await and the sky's the limit." Nothing could stop me now. A world of possibilities was on the map and I would learn to Sail Above The Clouds.

LESSON: S.A.I.L. Above The Clouds (Simplify, Align, Integrate, Let go). Illness and trauma takes a huge toll on our physical and emotional well-being. Being accepting and loving towards myself was a new way of being for me. I rediscovered what I liked and disliked and reconnected with my intuition. This helped me align my actions with what felt right in my heart, and allowed me to feel calmer and more confident about my decisions.

Mindfulness and meditation helped me reconnect with myself. It helped me move beyond overwhelming emotions and into the space of the wise self. Through reflection and journaling I was able to cut the drama around a given situation, and break it down to basics. It freed my mind to decide my next step. It shushed my inner critic, which at the time was overbearing and angry. It showed me how skewed my perception had been about my marriage and my relationships. It gave me a clean chart to plot out a new course.

In Meditative Writing, I found the answers I was searching for. I discovered a quiet space where my inner voice could learn to speak up. I cleared a path towards health and helping others on their healing journey. I gained confidence in my abilities and recognized that I had the power to heal my life all along. I discovered that I had been hiding behind walls of excuses and blame, and my body was only reacting in the only way it knew how to get my attention.

Simplifying my life helped me get to the core of what was ailing me, and it was much more than a debilitating illness. I sailed through hell and back, and lived through hurricanes before I found myself and gained the courage to claim who I wanted to be.

Life is an infinite canvas of greys in different shades, and we all use different sized paint brushes. Nothing is ever truly black or white, except the ego-mind which judges harshly. Mindfulness opened my mind's eye to a new canvas and a new horizon to paint.

It took a lot of work for me to get to where I am today–which is still a work in progress. I used all the tools in my S.A.I.L. program to reclaim my life.

I SIMPLIFIED my diet, my habits, my job, my relationships, and changed my inner drama to a bird's eye view of the grandeur picture.

I ALIGNED every aspect of my life with my goals and heart's purpose.

I INTEGRATED all the tools I learned to succeed.

I LEARNED TO LET GO of all that hindered my success: stress, worries, expectations, limited beliefs, and detrimental behaviors. I accepted that my body is human and loved it wholeheartedly just the way it was, without restrictions or judgments.

Simplifying is an art, for which sailors have a knack. And even when you think you've gotten as hardcore as possible, you can always go simpler. Did I tell you about our sailing friends who do the dishes with a spray bottle to save on carrying water?

THE END...

WHAT'S AHEAD?!

In **BOOK #2,** I share my journey on how I learned to **ALIGN MY GOALS WITH MY HEART'S PURPOSE.**

It includes:
- how to navigate in the dark when you don't know where you're going
- the hilarious "Dancing in the Galley" about cooking at sea and finding balance in life
- "Sex at Sea" hmm…yes, we have to talk about it!
- more laughs in, "Stop judging my flip-flops"
- an inspiring story of when we rescued stranded divers from imminent death
- "A close call with a Sea Monster"

You'll enjoy additional snapshots of my life on board, and find out how it feels to sleep and live on a floating vessel.

If you are searching for success and abundance, and struggle with all that you've tried, there is something out of alignment. If you are wondering about where your path lies, where to take your next step, what your purpose is, or have a hard time staying on course, then the exercises in Book #2 will help you get unstuck, give you tools to create a clear plan to reach your goals whether health, business or relationships. Alignment is a must for health and success!

BOOK #3 is jam-packed with adventures where I learned to **INTEGRATE TOOLS FOR SUCCESS.** You'll adventure into the time we almost sank in the Bahamas, climbing up the 50-foot mast, almost giving my mom a heart attack in stormy seas, dragging anchor in a surprise gale, how I became the witness to a man's last hour from a violent gun suicide, to lighter stories of pets on board, and dropping a truth bomb that may shock you.

If you are wondering how to manifest your vision and reach your goal, this book will help you explore how to integrate tools to have better relationships, build the discipline necessary to accomplish your goals, and establish a daily practice that supports your growth. If you're not using the tools in your treasure box, you won't be able to sustain an abundant healthy lifestyle.

In BOOK #4, I share about surviving the doldrums of a 30-year relationship on board a 41-foot vessel, sailing into alligator land, having a surreal burial at sea, being chased by a baby shark while naked, and sinking a dinghy which left us stranded on a deserted beach. I will recount the scariest day we've had on Windsong in 25 years. To give you a sneak peek, this was when we sailed up the East Coast from Florida to Maine and got caught in a dangerous 3.5 hour gale storm. We almost lost control of the boat, completely trashed it, almost caught fire, and I ended up having to abandon ship with a dorsal sprain—alone in a strange town. This forced me to dig deep, to survive the heartbreak of permanently moving off Windsong halfway on our trip in an unknown town. Here, I found myself homeless with my bags on the curb, feeling hurt, and alone. I had to find the strength to **LET GO** and trust that life would find a miraculous way of bringing Eric and I and Windsong back together to make everything alright again. I will also divulge a huge family secret I'd been carrying around for years.

Letting go is the ultimate act of freedom. It is the hardest thing to do, but the key to blissful peace and happiness. If you are experiencing resistance in any aspect of your life, there is something that needs to be LET GO. Read this book and try the exercises to help you achieve a level of surrender that will benefit your whole wellbeing. In learning to trust yourself, you will gain a whole new level of self-acceptance and fulfillment.

FREE

If you like the book and want to continue on this journey, stay onboard by signing up for my newsletter at www.SailAboveTheClouds.com. You'll be the first to know when Book #2, *Sail Above the Clouds too: ALIGN Your Goals with Purpose*, comes out—before it's launched publicly—and I'll email you the first chapter for FREE!

Please review this book!

Reviews help authors more than you might think. If you enjoyed *SAIL Above the Clouds*, please consider leaving a review at your Amazon or regular book store—it would be greatly appreciated—and may help Carole's stories sail towards unknown horizons!

...please share it with your friends...

...and don't forget to download your FREE meditation!

www.SailAboveTheClouds.com

About The Author

Carole sailed from Florida to Maine where she currently lives with her husband of 30-years. She enjoys discovering the vast nature that New England offers. She is a successful professional graphic designer, and continues her life-long study of holistic and yogic philosophies and learning ways of managing her health.

Carole is a certified Life Coach, Meditative Writing, Shakti Dance® Yoga, and Reiki Master Teacher. She teaches weekly online classes for stress-relief, mindfulness, yoga, and meditative writing (and when not in a pandemic, offers in-person classes at local studios).

She coaches and mentors women of all ages who seek inspiration and positive energy, so they can be proactive towards healing their bodies and minds to lead purposeful and healthier lives.

Find out more at www.inspiredlifebycarole.com and sign up for her newsletter for free helpful tips, life hacks, stories, and meditations.

Say Hello!

You can connect with Carole in a number of places. She inspires people every day on Facebook, through writing and uplifting shares, she visually entices on Instagram, she reviews and recommends her favorite books on Good Reads, and you can send her an email too. She welcomes your correspondence and will answer you personally.

Facebook: @InspiredCreationsInc
Instagram.com @awomaninspired
sailabovetheclouds@gmail.com

Journaling

_____

_____

_____

_____

_____

_____

_____

_____

_____

_____

_____

_____

_____

References

(1) Madhav Goyal, MD, MPH1; Sonal Singh, MD, MPH1; Erica
M. S. Sibinga, MD, MHS2, March 2014, *Meditation Programs for
Psychological Stress and Well-being - A Systematic Review and Meta-
analysis,* JAMA Network.

(2) Eileen Luders, Nicolas Cherbuin, and Florian Kurth, *Forever
Young(er): potential age-defying effects of long-term meditation on gray
matter atrophy,* 21 January 2015, Frontiers in Psychology.

(3) Judson A. Brewer, Patrick D. Worhunsky, Jeremy R. Gray, Yi-Yuan
Tang, Jochen Weber, and Hedy Kober, December 13, 2011, *Meditation
experience is associated with differences in default mode network
activity and connectivity,* Proceedings of the National Academy of
Sciences of the United States of America.

Made in the USA
Middletown, DE
17 January 2022

58849389R00146